As soon as we get this car gassed up, Russell and I are
going to find someone in Alaska to go pray for.

Albert, just a quick thank you note for your wonderful visit with us.
After I dropped you off at the airport in Fairbanks, I was on my way
home by 2 a.m. There is an old sourdough saying about Alaska and
the Northern Lights. It goes like this: "when a visitor leaves and the
Northern Lights are dancing that means you will be back.

I am overwhelmed every time I look at my right foot and see it the
same size as the left foot. When you prayed for me, I watched it grow.

Carol Dufendach

Embracing Adventure with Jesus

Revised Edition

Silver and gold have I none; but such as I have I give you: In the name of Jesus Christ of Nazareth rise up and walk. (Acts 3:6 KJV)

Embracing Adventure with Jesus

A Missionary Statesman
Who Impacted a Nation

Albert William Luepnitz

Embracing Adventure with Jesus – Albert William Luepnitz
Second edition Copyright © 2017
First edition published 2015

Scriptures marked KJV are from the King James Version.

Scriptures marked NKJV are from the Scripture taken from the New King James Version®. Copyright © 1982 by Thomas Nelson. Used by permission. All rights reserved.

Testimonies may have been edited for proper English.

Available wherever books are sold.

Cover Design: Natalia Hawthorne, BookCoverLabs.com
Background image: Chicamocha canyon, Wikipedia.org
eBook Icon: Icons Vector/Shutterstock

Printed in the United States of America
BIOGRAPHY & AUTOBIOGRAPHY / Religious
Paperback ISBN: 978-1-50895-128-5
eBook ISBN: 978-1-62245-275-0
10 9 8 7 6 5 4 3 2
Available where books are sold

Contents

Prologue

---◇---

One of God's most special gifts to me has been my friendship with Albert W. Luepnitz. We first met in the year 2009 at a gathering of senior military officers where Albert was the guest speaker and I was the photographer. During the event, Albert noticed I was slouching on one side as I was taking pictures. When he finished speaking, he approached me and asked if I had back problems. After suffering from a twisted back my whole life, when Albert prayed for me, I walked out of there with my spinal cord completely straightened and renewed. Little did I know then that this newfound friendship would give me a lot more than the healing of my back?

From that point on, we would see Albert every time he came to Colombia. After a few more visits, my whole family (literally) including my cousins, my grandma, uncles, aunts, even my niece and nephew, had been healed of similar hereditary back problems, which seemed to run rampant in our family. I accompanied Albert in a historic trip to Cuba and witnessed the power of God among the delegates of Colombia's peace negotiations taking place there.

Later on, in January 2014, I toured the southern and western mountains and jungles of Colombia as Albert's official translator. We visited everything from remote indigenous villages in the mountains to rich millionaires in the cities. Our tour lasted almost a month, and I was able to see many amazing miracles when Albert prayed for individuals. It was then that I could truly say that I had seen the blind healed and the lame begin to walk again. The power that Jesus had when He walked this earth did not pass away when He died, but is present today.

Even though I was seeing all these miracles, I was completely oblivious to the miracle that was taking place that would most affect my life. As I was translating for Albert, my future husband (who I had no clue would be my future husband) was watching every single miracle. He was this cute Alaskan guy who had come to Colombia to learn Spanish. We had been a little bit interested in each other when we met, but because he seemed to have no desire to follow the Lord, I wrote him off immediately. I ended up taking Albert to pray for my friends, right in the town where this Alaskan guy, Stephen Miller, had decided to study Spanish. Albert gave him a camera and told him to record everything he saw, which forced him to be with us. Stephen had a true encounter with the Lord in America ten years before, but lost his fervor when he realized that he knew no real disciples of Jesus Christ. However, he had made a promise to himself: If I ever meet a real disciple of Jesus Christ, I would follow the Lord with all my heart.

Ten years later, in a little town in the southern side of Colombia, he met Albert. There are many words that describe Albert, but I think Stephen describes him best when he says that Albert is one of Jesus' true disciples. It was that day, on January 17, 2014, after seeing days full of miracles, that Stephen could not deny it any longer. Now he knew that Albert was undeniably Jesus' disciple. Stephen was at a crossroads. Either he would continue to live his own life as he had been doing, or he would recognize this for what it was and keep his promise. After much conflict in his soul, Stephen decided to give his life over completely to the Lord Jesus and follow Him regardless of anything else he had wanted to do. He even put studying Spanish, something he had wanted to do for years, in God's hands. Before then he had been confused, thinking that following God was about being part of some organization or church, and that is why he hesitated and never committed.

But when Stephen met Albert, it was clear to him that true faith was not about following a certain leader or religion; it was about following the Lord Jesus wherever He may lead. The Lord Jesus is pure and will not lead us astray. Stephen and I got married in Alaska on August 17, 2014, exactly seven months after he gave his life over to the Lord, and Albert was one of our special guests. Stephen's family and the guests at the wedding were also very blessed by Albert's visit. Yes, many wonderful things have happened due to this special friendship. I can honestly say that my whole family has been miraculously healed and that I have seen incredible things that have strengthened my faith. And I am most grateful that God has given me a loving husband who truly respects me and wants to follow the Lord. It is because Stephen witnessed one of Jesus' true disciples walking the earth today: Albert.

– *Alethia Stendal*

Preface

This book is mainly about "Divine Encounters" that changed peoples' lives; often accompanied by prophecies, creative miracles, healings, and deliverance from demons. These happenings changed the lives of individuals as well as nations. They are the same phenomena narrated in the Gospels and duplicated in the Acts of the Apostles: the lame walk, the blind see, and the deaf hear. However, the Gospels also relate a number of punitive miracles in Acts. Most strikingly, Ananias and Sapphira are suddenly struck dead for having lied to the Holy Ghost; Herod is suddenly killed by an angel for arrogating to himself the honors due to God; and Saul is struck blind on his way to Damascus to kill Christians. This book refers to similar phenomenon. For example, in 1991 when the general of the armed forces of Colombia ordered that I could no longer minister on military bases in Colombia, within three weeks he suffered a massive stroke! Is this only a coincidence? Doubtful, as it was at a time when I was involved a major expansion of ministry throughout the armed forces. Later I received an invitation to return to the country.

The miracles performed by the apostles invoked the name of Jesus as a regular prelude to the occurrence and became our directive to do the same. This book also addresses the way in which unforgiveness can control emotions in a vice-like grip, in a prison without bars. This allows unhealthy thoughts to dominate our minds, a contributing factor in opening the door to physical and mental health problems. This was a controlling factor in my life until forgiveness unlocked the door, like an emotional shower, cleansing and freeing the entrapped soul. It can do the same for you. Jesus came to heal the brokenhearted and set the captives free. Accepting Jesus Christ as your Savior as well as forgiving yourself and others is the key that will open the door.

Introduction

In January 2013, Russell Martin Stendal told me that the Lord had directed him to use me to accompany him to the country of Cuba on a very important assignment. Russell has been ministering for over thirty years in Colombia, South America, and I have ministered with him since 2009.

The president of Colombia had asked the FARC (Revolutionary Armed Forces of Colombia) guerillas to discuss a peace agreement with a delegation from the Colombian government at a meeting in Cuba. At war with the government since 1964, the FARC have a substantial army and control a large area of Colombia. With their Marxist-Leninism ideology, they are Satanic-controlled militants desiring to overthrow the Colombian government. The FARC also deal in illegal drugs, with the main distribution in the United States and Europe. They have kidnapped thousands for ransom, killing pastors, missionaries, and most anyone following Jesus Christ. So many have been killed that in many areas of Colombia there is only one man for every six women.

I have ministered in Colombia since 1984, leading many thousands to Jesus and seeing miracle healings on all sides of this conflict. So, why did the Lord tell Russell to take me with him to Cuba? Russell and his daughter, Alethia, had witnessed for many years how I ministered to thousands of Colombians in the gifts of the Holy Spirit, mostly all creative miracle healings and deliverance of demons, in the name of Jesus. It became clear that only the demonstration of such power would make possible the needed impact on the FARC delegates, who happened to also be their main leaders. Therefore, in answer to Russell's prayer, the Lord told him to take me, Albert.

The objective was to get the FARC leadership to be receptive to establishing peace in Colombia.

We met with the FARC delegation, one of whom had helped get Russell released from captivity in 1983. I eventually prayed for healing of a FARC woman named Maritza and everyone present witnessed when her left shoulder and incredibly deformed right foot, injured when a mine she stepped on exploded, were totally healed in the name of Jesus. It was evident that demons were also being delivered from those present. The change in facial expressions was easy to see as their mask of darkness left.

Quickly we understood that this was the beginning of witnessing one of the most profound displays of miracle healing that only the Lord could do; it was a true demonstration in the authority of the name of Jesus and the power of the Holy Spirit. There was no question that it had an immediate effect on the FARC leadership, who displayed their exuberant happiness on that occasion. We prayed for others, including their leader, Ivan.

The creative miracle healing of Maritza, I believe, was the moment of truth for the FARC guerrillas as it was the evidence they could not deny. The authority in the name of Jesus and the power of the Holy Spirit was superior to anything they had ever seen or experienced.

One other very important happening took place. The FARC delegates soon realized that Russell and I were trustworthy and therefore acceptable for future meetings with them.

Then Russell had a long teaching session with them; and

the following evening, with tears flowing, their leader, Ivan Marquez, told us that now they knew God loved them too. They made a clear decision to accept Jesus Christ and voiced their desire for peace in Colombia.

During the following two years, I prayed for most all of the FARC top command (Secretariat) and many secondary leaders. All received miracle healings, accepted Jesus, and wanted peace in Colombia.

In April 2013, I had a word for the FARC organization and the president of Colombia: "that the killing had to stop, that the peace treaty had to be settled God's way, not man's way or it would fail, and that if it failed, there would be major consequences." The FARC leadership accepted this prophecy. However, it took two more years and many meetings to make this a reality.

At the end of 2014, peace talks were taking place between the highest levels of both sides, and results appeared favorable.

Russell Martin Stendal and his daughter Alethia are the authors of a book, *The Hidden Agenda,* which explains details of the extraordinary true story behind Colombia's peace negotiations. Albert and others are the *"hidden agenda"* that these hardened, demon-controlled guerrillas were confronted with.

The Call: Early Ministry

---

*They overcame him by the blood of the Lamb, and by
the word of their testimony.* (Revelation 12:11 KJV)

In April 1981, I awoke two mornings in a row and heard what
seemed like an audible voice saying, "I made you financially
secure. I trained you in many things. I want you to help the
needy and the poor, to spread the gospel and work for *me*." I
thought I was hallucinating and mentioned it to my wife, Jean.

Jean and I had recently moved from Dallas to Longview,
Texas. I was suffering from what I was told was an untreat-
able back condition and facing the prospects of shortly being
in a wheelchair to get around. Jean had to assist me in about
everything I did.

I had served in the US Army for over twenty-four years
mainly as a special agent with the Criminal Investigation
Division, followed by being a fraud investigator in Dallas. I
also made real estate investments.

In May 1981, my brother Carl informed me of a woman from
Longview that had spoken at a Full Gospel Fellowship meeting
in Temple, Texas. This woman apparently had a miracle-healing
ministry. He suggested I see her.

Jean drove me to see her. She placed her hand on me, spoke

healing in the name of Jesus, and I was healed. Jean had an issue of blood. We had not told her of this problem, but she said the Lord told her. She spoke healing in the name of Jesus, and Jean received her healing. In addition, Jean and I received the fullness of the Holy Spirit, known as the baptism in the Holy Spirit with speaking in tongues.

I knew that what we had just experienced was in conflict with all teaching I had received in every church I had ever attended. They had taught that the gifts of the Holy Spirit mentioned in 1 Corinthians 12, including speaking in tongues, had died out with the last Apostles.

Immediately I knew that *God did love me*, which was a complete reverse of what I had always believed. Then I felt like something was falling off me, and I realized that the inconceivable had happened. I not only received a physical healing, but the hard shell that encompassed me, holding in my trauma from childhood, suppressed emotions, a hardness of heart from childhood and military duties – in a prison without bars – suddenly broke off. For the first time in over forty years, I experienced what Jesus said, *"The Spirit of the Lord is upon me, because … he hath sent me to heal the brokenhearted, to preach deliverance to the captives"* (Luke 4:18 KJV). And I cried, I cried, and I cried some more. It was the beginning of inner healing. I knew God had a call on my life, and it was not just a hallucination.

Going through the Cleansing Fire

For several months, my wife Jean and I assisted the woman that had prayed for our healings in completing a building project. A prophecy had been spoken over me that the Lord was going to use me in the gifts of healings, and I would become known as an *Ambassador of Peace to Nations.*

Jean and I enrolled in a video course from Charles and

Frances Hunter's School of Ministry, to study the Bible, with a focus on operating in the gifts of the Holy Spirit. We completed this course about a year later. The Hunters also had a highly regarded healing ministry throughout the world. In addition, we had the pleasure of hearing many guest speakers and were exposed to learning not only the Word, but applying the Word for inner healing and physical healing.

In 1981, Jean and I were attending Saint Michael and All Angel's Episcopal Church in Longview, Texas. They aspired to build a fellowship hall, to accommodate an addition to the church sanctuary for classrooms, a kitchen, and other activities. I asked the priest, Father Walter Ellis, if I could see the definitive drawings (blueprints) of the proposed construction. The building contractors estimated the cost of the project at approximately $400,000, which the church could not afford. When I examined the documents, I realized that the building was identical to one in Irving, Texas, that I built about six months previously for $140,000. I told Ellis about this. Actually, at the time I had no idea of the reality of such a project, but I had a gut feeling. A few months after I received my miracle healing, Ellis contacted me and told me the vestry had approved the idea but wanted to know more about it. I briefed them and they were satisfied. The presiding bishop in Houston, Texas, also gave his approval. Today, I still smile as no one ever bothered to ask me if I was a contractor.

I will make a long story short. It took thirteen months to complete and it gave me insight what the Lord wanted to teach me. I went over the blueprints with the architect and obtained his full cooperation. The next step was getting a contractor to do the dirt work. When that was supposedly finished, I noticed that the architect had made a mistake as to the height of the dirt. Because of the slope of the adjacent land, water would enter the building. In thinking about it, I made a comment to myself; *I wonder how high the dirt has to be.* I immediately heard, like a quiet thought, to raise it seven and one-quarter inches. The dirt contractor and the architect both asked how high, as they said they could not determine it. I told them, "Seven and a quarter inches." They asked, "How do you know?" And I told them the Lord told me. This was really my first experience that I knew I was hearing from the Lord. I followed the direction of that same voice every time I needed a construction answer. From that day on, *He* was my guide to complete the building. I received *His* guidance in locating contractors that were happy to subcontract at their cost, for a specific building project, to keep their workers employed between other jobs. They completed the concrete, framing, roof, brick, plumbing, and electrical work at a fraction of the normal cost. Church volunteers helped in painting and other areas. I personally constructed some of the building.

When construction was about half completed, Father Ellis said he had something to tell me. At the time I mentioned about the gut feeling, he was in daily prayer for several weeks. He asked the Lord to send someone to build the parish hall at a price they could afford. "*The effectual fervent prayer of a righteous man availeth much*" (James 5:16 KJV). We completed the building at a cost of $140,000, exactly the amount I thought when I was having the gut feeling.

Learning to Forgive
The Lord Dispatched Me on a Special Mission
After I finished building the fellowship building, I heard the Lord tell me, "I want you to go to Moran, Michigan where you grew up, on a special mission." I asked, "Who should I see?" He told me to see Vernon Erskine.

My wife and I immediately left on the 3,000-mile-round-trip journey, arriving on a Friday afternoon. I telephoned Vernon and he asked me to come to his home at 3 p.m. the following day (Saturday).

At 3 p.m. Saturday, I arrived and told Vernon the Lord told me to see him, but I did not know why. We visited awhile and he suggested a meeting the following Tuesday evening where I could meet many of the folks I grew up with.

On Tuesday evening, there were about thirty present. I knew most of them and they were happy to see me. I told them what had occurred in my life and about what the Lord was doing. All wanted prayer for healing and many were healed.

The last one asking for prayer was a young girl. She said, "Albert, you don't know me, but you saved my life." She related that last Saturday at 3 p.m., her father, Vernon, was watching television, her mother had gone shopping, and she was in the kitchen thinking about committing suicide by cutting her wrists. When she heard me tell her dad why I was there, she changed her mind. I prayed for her and she accepted Jesus. She has grown up now, a wonderful person set free.

What is interesting about this story is I was expelled from school in 1943 when in the tenth grade, blamed for an injury to another student named Leonard that I knew nothing about. No one would believe me. I actually had hated most of my former classmates that I just prayed for, as I felt they did not speak up for me with the truth. When I talked with them, I realized how happy they were to see me and I forgave them. Some present at the meeting actually knew the truth but had been afraid to mention it.

Years later, I located Leonard's address and wrote a short letter, forgiving him for what he did. I received a reply from his wife. She said Leonard had died five years previously of cancer; he was a wonderful husband and father and loved their children. Also, she related that his father was a lot like mine and Leonard had been afraid to tell his dad the truth.

I learned something from this. Think about the fact you might be wrong about what you think. I gave a message on a CD to the FARC leadership about how I had been wrong about Leonard. I asked them to think about the fact that they may be wrong about their political views. There is a better way. They listened to this CD message many times and they have changed.

I had numerous meetings over the years in Moran and saw many healed. In one meeting, a mother asked me to pray for her son who was facing major surgery. His lower jaw extended about a three-quarter inch longer than the upper jaw. The mother said the upper jaw had not fully developed. I commanded in the name of Jesus that the upper jaw grow and be even with the lower jaw. It did.

There was one thing I was not able to do. I could not forgive my dad or forget the horrible beatings he gave most of us, including my mother. He would go crazy with anger, beating to death his farm animals for no logical reason. I could not stand being in Moran for more than a few days because of the depression and memories. It took several years before I was able to forgive him but only when the Lord showed me why my father was like he was.

When I was in the third grade, my brother, Otto, threw a stick that pierced my right eye. Dad would not take me to a doctor. The pain was awful and I became blind in that eye. Then apparently the infection set in and I was also going blind in my left eye. My teacher would not believe me that I could not see the blackboard even just a few feet from it. Her punishment for lying was putting a piece of soap in my mouth with tape over my mouth and standing me in a corner for hours. Then she would tell Dad, who was the bus driver, how I lied, which always resulted in another beating. I flunked the third grade. The following school year I had a new teacher. I told her my problem. She really got after Dad about it. He took me to a doctor, who told Dad that, because of the severe infection, in another three months I would have been blind for life. I recovered the sight in my left eye but remained blind in my right. Many years later, surgery restored some sight to my right eye. How do you forgive an experience like that? Well, I did.

Forgiving was one thing; forgetting the hurts was another. About 2009, the Lord showed me what would help: to think of one good thing my dad did. It wasn't long before I recalled a lot of good he did. Then I was to see happy faces on my relatives instead of sadness. I refused to think or dwell on the past.

My memories of old faded away and now I have good memories. No more depression or anxiety when visiting Moran.

How I Learned to Forgive My Dad

I had been ministering for several years throughout North and South America, seeing many thousands healed and accepting Jesus. I was also a frequent guest speaker at many of the Full Gospel Businessmen's Fellowship International conventions, closing the conventions with a Saturday evening healing service.

In about 1987, I was at a convention in San Antonio, Texas, that lasted several days. I had the Saturday evening meeting and healing service. On Friday, a US Army four-star general asked me to have breakfast with him Saturday morning.

While having breakfast we talked for a while when he suddenly asked me, "What are you going to speak on tonight?" I said, "Insubordination." The general replied, "That should be a very interesting message." In the military, we all knew the seriousness of this; disobedience to an order was followed by discipline.

I went to my hotel room and walked the floor, telling myself, *why did you say that?* Suddenly I heard the Lord speak to me. It was like a thought but very clear:

I am going to show you how to forgive your dad and that is what you are to speak on tonight.

I saw a vision, something like on a black-and-white TV screen. On it was a picture illustrating my family history on my Dad's side, of a decanting demon of anger from my grandfather, to Dad, to my brother Otto. He also exhibited a lot of extreme anger while we were growing up but seemed better years later. He died at age forty-two.

The Lord made it very clear to me that all three relatives were victims, controlled by a demon of anger that they inherited from previous generations.

When shown that Dad was a victim of something he did not understand or knew how to get rid of, I was suddenly overwhelmed with grief and forgave him. Dad had died years ago, October 22, 1951, on my birthday.

Also, the Lord made it clear to me that I was insubordinate toward my dad on many occasions. The Word says, *"Honor your father and your mother … that your days may be long"* Deuteronomy 5:16 NKJV).

I gave about a forty-minute message that Saturday night. The anointing of the Holy Spirit was so strong that people could not get near the podium. They were going down under the power of the Holy Spirit, including the four-star general.

I witnessed one of the most awesome displays of how the Lord healed the broken hearted and set over four hundred individuals free. I heard the short testimonies of many as they left, verifying their inner healing, and I have conveyed this message to thousands throughout North and South America.

Albert by faith forgave.

Unforgiveness and God's Judgment

Therefore I say to you, whatever things you ask when you pray, believe that you receive them and you will have them. And whenever you stand praying, if you have anything against anyone, forgive him, that your Father in heaven may also forgive you your trespasses. But if you do not forgive, neither will your Father in heaven forgive your trespasses. (Mark 11:24-26) See also Matthew 6:15 and Colossians 3:13 NKJV

Unforgiveness leaves the Father no choice but to turn you over to the torturers (Satan).

The Parable of the Unforgiving Servant

Then Peter came to Him and said, "Lord, how often shall my brother sin against me, and I forgive him? Up to seven times?"

Jesus said to him, "I do not say to you, up to seven times, but up to seventy times seven.* Therefore the kingdom of heaven is like a certain king who wanted to settle accounts with his servants. And when he

had begun to settle accounts, one was brought to him who owed him ten thousand talents. But as he was not able to pay, his master commanded that he be sold, with his wife and children and all that he had, and that payment be made. The servant therefore fell down before him, saying, 'Master, have patience with me, and I will pay you all.' Then the master of that servant was moved with compassion, released him, and forgave him the debt.

"But that servant went out and found one of his fellow servants who owed him a hundred denarii; and he laid hands on him and took him by the throat, saying, 'Pay me what you owe!' So his fellow servant fell down at his feet and begged him, saying, 'Have patience with me, and I will pay you all.' And he would not, but went and threw him into prison till he should pay the debt. So when his fellow servants saw what had been done, they were very grieved, and came and told their master all that had been done. Then his master, after he had called him, said to him, 'You wicked servant! I forgave you all that debt because you begged me. Should you not also have had compassion on your fellow servant, just as I had pity on you?' And his master was angry, and delivered him to the torturers until he should pay all that was due to him.

"So My heavenly Father also will do to you if each of you, from his heart, does not forgive his brother his trespasses." (Matthew 18:21-35 NKJV)

This is the root cause of much emotional and physical oppression. It will most certainly guarantee that in most cases deliverance and healing, if it even happens, will be only temporary.

NOTE: 70 x 7 is a number combination that Biblically carries a special meaning – "complete restoration."

Unforgiveness and Unclean or Bitter Spirits

"When an unclean spirit goes out of a man, he goes through dry places, seeking rest, and finds none. Then he says, 'I will return to my house from which I came.' And when he comes, he finds it empty, swept, and put in order. Then he goes and takes with him seven other spirits more wicked than himself, and they enter and dwell there; and the last state of that man is worse than the first. So shall it also be with this wicked generation." (Matthew 12:43-45 NKJV)

The consequences of unforgiveness or an unclean spirit is evident in almost every couple or individual seeking counsel. This is most common, most basic sin in marital relationships. And it's usually the consequence of having judged a parent or parents in violation of the first commandment with a promise: "'*Honor your father and mother,' which is the first commandment with promise"* (Ephesians 6:2 NKJV) combined with "*Judge not, that you be not judged, for with what judgment you judge, it will be measured back to you*" (Matthew 7: 1-5 NKJV). What does this mean? It means that you or your spouse can become a mirror of the parent you judged. I have never seen a marriage restored if forgiveness of a parent is not dealt with.

In one instance, a woman had a nasty rash on her shoulders and neck. Her husband said the rash developed and got worse when his wife started complaining bitterly after an operation, believing the doctors had overcharged her. I prayed for her but nothing happened. She agreed and expressed forgiveness of the doctors. Later her husband called me and said the rash left in about two days. About a month later, he called me again. His wife was again very bitter at the doctors and the rash returned. Her bitterness increased to involve more than the doctors and resulted in getting a divorce. She died about a year later.

Another case, the parents of a fifteen-year-old boy brought him to my office for prayer. They explained that a few months previously, he had become partially paralyzed in his right leg and it was twisted. Several doctors had failed to find the reason nor were able to treat him. I decided to talk to him without his parents present. I discerned he had a serious problem with forgiveness and confronted him. He related that there was a girl he cared for but she moved to another city when her dad was transferred. One day she called and said she was pregnant, blaming him. This boy said he was not the father but he became very bitter. However, he did admit that he introduced her to mutual satisfaction and had started her on a course that got out of control. Well, when he forgave her and himself, he walked out of my office healed.

In a convention meeting in Tyler, Texas, one of many miracle healings was a woman with a clubfoot. Some of us, including me, were standing in a hallway where people were exiting the meeting. As this woman was leaving, her husband came up to her and asked, "You will forgive me now, won't you dear?" She snapped back, "Yes, I will forgive you." We saw the clubfoot condition immediately return.

A doctor friend asked me to meet him. One of his female patients was blind. When I prayed for her, she was totally healed of the blindness. About three months later, this doctor called me and said the woman had lost her healing and was again blind. He explained that the woman's daughter came home for a visit and was very angry at her mother for letting those "tongue talkers" pray for her. Several days of this and her mother became blind again. We prayed for healing again but this time there was no healing.

In Naples, Florida, I was ministering at a church with about fifty people in attendance. These individuals all had facial expressions that looked like extreme stress or pain. I stopped speaking and asked the pastor, "What has happened here? Why are these people so unhappy?" The pastor said that three months previously the youth pastor left, taking all the young people with him, starting a new church of his own.

I questioned the remaining members and found something very interesting. I noticed that since the church split, those that already had arthritis found the pain and symptoms had increased. Those without arthritis before the split found that they had developed arthritis joint pain symptoms. Every remaining person who stayed after the split acknowledged that they harbored bitterness, anger, and unforgiveness. After I gave a Bible-based message on the reason for their new problems, they all verbalized forgiving the ones who had left.

About six months later, I was again in Naples and visited the pastor. He told me most of all the remaining individuals were healed or much better.

About 1990 I was asked by a church in Florida if I would teach at a Bible missionary training school in La Paz, Bolivia. I agreed, but before leaving the Lord told me there was going to be a pastors' conference in La Paz and that I would be asked to speak to them. I was to tell them: "I gave you a vision, but you got it out of focus." About two weeks in La Paz, a pastor came to the school and asked me if I would address their pastors' conference. I did and after speaking about ten minutes, a pastor asked if I had a word from the Lord for them. I told them what the Lord told me to tell them. They all started crying and after a few minutes gathered around a person on one side of the room. My interpreter said they were asking forgiveness from a person that had started a tent ministry. The more upset they had become, the more the church attendance had diminished until over two thirds had left. After they asked forgiveness, I spoke at many of their churches. The attendance not only returned, but increased.

I have prayed for many with similar stories when ministering throughout North and South America. The only solution to solve these cases is asking the Lord to forgive you.

You do not lose your peace with God because of someone else's sin, but as a result of your own sin. Unforgiveness is sin.

> *There is therefore no condemnation to those who are in Christ Jesus, who do not walk according to the flesh, but according to the Spirit.*
> (Romans 8:1 NKJV)

Report from Carl Luepnitz

—◇—

O n November 2ⁿᵈ, 1980, while in evening prayer, I had a vision of a long-hand note that read, "On November seventh, your brother was killed." I became so anxious I forgot to see which brother's name was on the note. I had two brothers. I continued in prayer and the Lord said, "Get out of Guadalajara," and I thought of a place called Rincon de Guiabedes, about four hours away. This was in Mexico. We went the next day, rented a bungalow, and both Helen and I went into prayer at the side of the bed. The Lord said the brother was Albert and we began interceding for him. I committed him to do anything the Lord desired of him, only spare his life. I asked that as many angels as needed be dispatched to change the circumstances. After two hours of intercession the Lord indicated that because of our intercession the circumstances were changed and Albert's life was spared.

When we returned to Guadalajra, I telephoned Albert. He said a man stated he was going to shoot him.

Later I received word that Albert was going to share his testimony at the Full Gospel Businessmen's Fellowship International in Temple, Texas. (This was about six months later.) I drove to McAllen, and a friend flew me in a small aircraft to Temple. It was extremely dangerous flying, as most of the way was violent thunderstorms. It was a scary trip and landing.

That evening I heard Albert share his testimony where he stated he had become very depressed as the doctors told him he would never get out of a wheelchair. He was dejected with his life; however, he remembered that I had told him of a woman evangelist with a powerful anointing that lived in his area. He visited her and was healed and received the baptism of the Holy Spirit. They also told him to get a pencil and paper and write down the mission the Lord gave him. A mission was to act as a general contractor and build a large building for a church in Longview, Texas. This was in 1980. Since then the Lord gave him many missions and he still, in 2014, is working at eighty-nine years of age as an ambassador for the Lord in South America and other places.

By faith Albert accepts a mission to build a church
and also to become an ambassador for the Lord.

Changing Direction

Wher my wife, Jean, and I received our miracle healings, we were overjoyed with love and appreciation for the person that prayed for us. We volunteered to assist her in building her ministry facility. It was a joy to do so and very much a learning experience, not only from observing her meetings but the numerous guest speakers she invited over a period of seven months.

This woman asked me to look after her facility while she was absent and to continue certain building projects. Jean and I did so, putting in ten-hour days and many evenings when she had services.

Then one Saturday, we received the shock of our lives. This woman, very angry, with her husband, came by our home and falsely accused us of having healing services at her facility while she was absent. She would not accept that it was not true and told us she no longer wanted us at her facility. Someone she highly trusted told her a lie. She believed it and still does to this day, over thirty years later. She is still a highly regarded Christian television personality with some good messages.

It was then that the building of the parish hall for a church as previously explained developed. When that building project was completed after thirteen months, which was all volunteer time for me, I was to meet with the leaders of the church. I called the vestry, giving them a final briefing. To my surprise, most were smoking, which makes me very sick. I asked them if they could stop smoking for a half hour. With a very angry response, one of them replied, "If you don't like it, why don't you just leave?" None of the others responded, but kept smoking. I had no choice but to leave. There was no, "Thank you, Albert," just a severely bruised spirit. Later there was a small celebration where I was presented a ring. This resulted in another change of direction.

I had become friends with the pastor of another church in Longview and started attending. This was where I belonged. I was totally accepted and it was where my ministry developed. Coinciding with meetings throughout North and South America, for over fifteen years, I gave many Word-based counseling seminaries and healing services at this church. I left this church for personal reasons that had nothing to do with them. My wife, Jean, had died and I found it difficult to be without her; I also moved to a different location.

I have written this chapter for one reason only. I found that I could easily have become complacent at each place described and there remained. But it was not in the Lord's plan for my life, just intermediate training grounds.

Looking back, I can see that the Lord had to slam a door totally closed in my face in order to get me to change to where I am now.

Ministry in Lima, Peru

In about 1983, I was a director with the Longview, Texas, chapter of the Full Gospel Businessmen's Fellowship International. The Longview chapter president, Joe McCracken, and I, along with an international director, went to Lima, Peru, for what was known as an airlift to assist in establishing chapters.

We had just finished checking in at the Sheridan Hotel in Lima and were still at the counter when an individual came in and showed us a paper with my name on it. He was identified as a Peruvian Indian Christian pastor from an area some distance from Lima. My interpreter was a Bible translator from Canada. The Indian did not speak English and only spoke limited Spanish. My interpreter said he thought the Indian wanted the baptism of the Holy Spirit, apparently the reason he came to see me. He didn't seem to understand anything we attempted to converse with him on, like, "How did you get my name?"

Suddenly I started speaking in a strange language. The Indian raised his hands above his head and appeared to answer me. I recognized I had been speaking in his language. His language suddenly changed and it was obvious he received what he came for.

He gave the name of a local hospital and we decided that was where he wanted to go. When we arrived at the hospital, we went to a ward where there were many Indian children. As the Indian prayed for these children, we were told they all were being treated for heartworm. No one could find out how he got my name or how he knew where to find me.

We were very successful in meeting local businessmen and organized a number of chapters.

The prospect of receiving a miracle healing from the Lord drew large numbers of people and many were healed, including a woman named Angela, who became my interpreter.

One of these meetings consisted of about two hundred senior local bank officials. We each shared a short testimony to this group. They didn't seem impressed when I spoke. I shared about the miracle healing I had received and what I was seeing in others I prayed for.

A woman left the meeting but returned shortly with a young girl. Her right leg since birth was bent at the knee, locked in that position. I placed my hand on her knee, commanded in the name of Jesus for the devil to release her. With a noise that could be heard by all, the leg immediately straightened. Everyone there, including the two bank guards, accepted Jesus.

This group formed a banker's chapter of the Full Gospel Businessmen's Fellowship International and I understand they are still meeting.

President Fernando Belaunde Terry invited me for a meeting with him and some of his staff. The president discussed some very serious national security problems he wanted prayer for, one of which was the growing number of rebel forces in Peru. (I thought about the prophecy spoken over me that the Lord was going to use me as an ambassador of peace to many nations.)

The president introduced me to a member of his staff and directed them to arrange a meeting with all branches of the national government.

These meetings took several days. I spent many hours praying for members of the Supreme Court, the national police commander and all their staff, and other federal branches of the government. In every branch, many with serious health issues were prayed for and received miracle healings. Many others accepted Jesus.

My interpreter at other meetings was a young woman named Angela. Hundreds were healed of various needs including her. One of them at a church meeting was a little baby girl that did not appear to have bones in her legs.

A nurse from the United States embassy in Lima asked to see me. She asked if I could pray for all the embassy staff, including civilian staff from Peru. The ambassador was not present, but I met the deputy ambassador who gave approval. The nurse was correct. Many had health issues. I prayed for them and they were healed. One very unusual case was a civilian employee who was in the hospital with a disease that caused all his joints to become rigid and inflexible.

I commanded in the name of Jesus that the condition reverse itself, that the joints function normally. The man first moved his arms and legs. He got out of bed and walked around. A few minutes later, he was doing push-ups at which time his doctor came into the room, followed by a number of medical students. He asked what was going on. The nurse told the doctor, the Lord just healed his patient. We left and returned to the embassy.

I ministered in Lima later, establishing chapters and healing services. The stories of the thousands that accepted Jesus and who were delivered of demons and healed is too much to detail. And we give all glory to the Lord.

By faith Albert became an ambassador of peace.

Testimony by Angela Hirst

I was Albert's interpreter on many occasions in Lima, Peru, when I resided there in the 1980s.

Wow, Al! What a life full of adventure you have! Praise the Lord! I recall seeing many miracles of healing and deliverance (in Lima) that the Lord did through your hands. At that time, I thought it was just how Christianity should look. There was a boy who was about eight months old that had not moved his legs since birth and his legs were limp. After you laid hands on him and prayed, the little boy started moving his legs. In addition, a girl about eight years old had her feet turned inward. You prayed and then told her to walk. As she started walking her feet started to straighten up until they were perfectly straight.

I had scoliosis of the spine and was having pains when I woke up every morning, so much so that I had to roll out of bed onto the floor and then slowly get up. When you checked my spine, you said that one shoulder was higher than the other one. When you prayed, I felt the power of the Holy Spirit working in my body and making it twist and turn. I knew the Lord was doing it. I guess He was adjusting my vertebrae, and when He was done, my spine was perfectly straight, I thought, as the back of a ballerina. I have not had any back pain since. That was over thirty years ago.

It was glorious! I was living as a believer only about two or three months. What a way to start my Christian walk. I feel privileged to have been able to witness so many miracles.

A Word from the Full Gospel Businessmen's Fellowship International

---

I n 1984, when I was a member of the Full Gospel Businessmen's Fellowship International, I was asked to share a short testimony at their world convention.

Some of the national directors heard me and told me that the Lord had prompted each of them that I was to make a tour of South America to assist in starting chapters in the various countries. I agreed. I went to many countries, starting with Brazil. Many new chapters were formed in every country, and the increase in membership of established chapters was in the thousands. The many miracle healings were a major factor in this growth.

When my wife and I arrived in Quito, Ecuador, we were met at the air terminal by a chapter president and some others. My wife left to go where we were staying and I was taken to a meeting room at a very plush hotel. The room was full of mainly very well-dressed men and women. I gave a testimony, as was common with this organization, prayed for several, and suddenly noticed that some were starting to go through deliverance. I requested they all come up to the front as there was a tile floor versus nice carpeting in the seating area. It was obvious to me most were heaving up demons. After about half an hour one of the men said to me in English, "Albert, do you know who we are?" I replied, "You are businessmen." He said, "No, we are all mainline-denomination preachers for Ecuador and did not know a Christian could have a demon." He said, "You have totally changed our theology in Ecuador that a Christian could not have a demon." (Please note: These individuals were not demon possessed, only oppressed by a demon.)

I was invited to minister at several local churches and the Christ for the World School in Quito. One of the staff members at the school was an American that knew my brother while training for mission work at Christ for the Nations in Dallas, Texas. There were about 150 students, and while I was teaching and ministering, every student went through a major deliverance. Several then gave a short testimony identifying the nature of the demons and a theory as to why the oppression. The school staff was shocked, telling me for years they had unsuccessfully tried to do deliverance. I was asked to give a teaching on deliverance to the staff. The main teaching of course is to address and eliminate the legal reason they have a demon, such as anger, unforgiveness, or whatever. I gave them a copy of the prayers I use to accomplish this.

By faith Albert dealt with demons that oppress.

Colombia and the Colonel

---∽---

The last country was Colombia, where it was arranged for me to meet Colonel Armando Cifuentes Espinosa, head of Colombian Military Intelligence. He had already started a chapter and had been named a national director. He arranged for me to stay at the "Club Military" officer's quarters on a military base in Bogotá. The night before my arrival, the rebel forces, FARC, had attacked the base and had blown off a portion of the roof where I was to stay! The first meeting was at a dinner at a local restaurant where I was the guest speaker. When I was introduced, I stood up at the podium and looked out at the gathering of soldiers and civilians, and saw what was identical to a vision the Lord gave me before leaving the United States. I had seen similar groups in other countries, but not this exact vision. I then heard the Lord speak to me, "This is where you are to minister from now on – Colombia." Many were healed and accepted Jesus in this meeting, but I heard prayer requests that I had never heard before.

There were an incredible number of loved ones being held for ransom by the FARC guerillas; and children leaving home to become guerrillas.

Colonel Cifuentes briefed me about a war that had been going on in Colombia since 1964. In 1984, this rebel organization called FARC (Revolutionary Armed Forces of Colombia), controlled over three-thirds of the country and dedicated itself to overthrowing the Colombian government. The FARC, long involved in cocaine production and kidnapping for ransom, had captured and/or killed all the pastors, missionaries, and envoys preaching Jesus Christ. The enticement of becoming a guerrilla was a big attraction and they recruited many young teenagers.

The following day, Colonel Cifuentes took me to a Colombian military hospital in Bogotá. We were in a ward of thirty wounded soldiers. One was blind; others had holes of missing flesh caused by shrapnel, gunshots wounds, and broken bones – all the evidence of serious combat. I prayed for all these wounded soldiers and many were healed. They were very busy taking off bandages and casts. Most of these soldiers left the room and returned shortly with wounded soldiers from throughout the hospital. At least three hundred soldiers were healed that day. Colonel Cifuentes, the doctors, and my wife were sitting on a bed crying. When I was alone I, too cried. This confirmed to me that the Lord was serious that my main mission duties were to be in Colombia.

For over twenty-five years I prayed for wounded soldiers at military hospitals and Colombian bases all over Colombia with many healed, but some were not. I also addressed the graduating class of newly commissioned officers, with the main subject being why they needed Jesus to be a good officer.

This was interrupted briefly in 1991 when the commanding general of Colombian forces ordered Colonel Cifuentes not to allow me on any more military bases or hospitals. Three weeks later, this general had a massive stroke. The newly appointed general rescinded the order.

Witchcraft in Colombia

The FARC guerrillas and drug cartel have been in rebellion against the Colombian government since 1964. The Word says, "*Rebellion is as the sin of witchcraft*" (1 Samuel 15:23).

I was in Colombia only a short time when injured Colombian soldiers were telling me about mental problems and thoughts of suicide. This continued for many years, usually about one out of the six injured soldiers at the main hospital facilities in Bogotá related this!

In June 2004, I started asking questions like, "What do you mean by mental problems?" Many of them emphasized that the rebels were putting witchcraft curses on them. This really got my attention. I had just failed to see a blind soldier and a deaf soldier healed. I asked the Lord for direction. His instructions were: "Break the witchcraft curse of blindness and deafness on these soldiers, in the name of Jesus." So I bound the curse of blindness and commanded it to leave in the name of Jesus. One of the men was instantly healed. I did the same for the deaf soldier. He started screaming – obviously in extreme pain. I told him to place his finger in each ear and command: "In the name of Jesus," over and over. This went on for about ten minutes and suddenly he was completely delivered as the pain left and he regained his hearing. From then on, I started addressing the mental problems as a deliverance problem as the Lord directed. Colonel Cifuentes was present at most of these meetings and was aware of this situation.

In May 2005, I went to Medellin, Colombia, and was taken directly from the airport to a restaurant for dinner and a meeting with Full Gospel Businessmen's Fellowship International, to be briefed about my meetings starting the following day. At this restaurant, a woman approached me and told me she was a witch and it had taken her seven hours to get there from the rebel-controlled area. She said she wanted deliverance. (The following day we accompanied her on the request.) I asked her how she knew where to meet me and why we were to meet? She said the rebels had a network of witches that kept up with me and always know where I am, to disrupt my meetings. She said her husband had forced her to leave her home following many disagreements. He was a powerful witch and was one of the main ones putting curses on the Colombian Army. She confirmed what the soldiers were telling me in Bogotá, telling me all about it. Over the years, Russell and I both noticed a decrease in the effectiveness of witches on the Colombian Army as a result of their acceptance of our respective ministry with them.

I had learned years ago that before any meetings, I was to command, in the name of Jesus, that any witchcraft assignments against me would reverse themselves and return to the sender. When I would enter the facility for meetings I had to laugh when, usually women, would jump up and run out.

I applied the Word: *"For though we walk in the flesh, we do not war according to the flesh"* (2 Corinthians 10:3 NKJV). The problem in Colombia is not just normal battle, but also spiritual warfare. By the time I went to Cuba you can be sure that God had equipped me with spiritual knowledge to handle this.

By faith Albert commanded the spirit of
witchcraft and curses were broken.

Testimonies

Dr. Lilana Castellanos Vivas

During several years, from approximately 2004 to 2008, I had the privilege and honor to serve as an interpreter at many meetings for Albert Luepnitz in Bogotá, Colombia; especially at the military facility where injured soldiers were treated for combat-related injuries in our internal war with revolutionary forces. In each meeting there would be approximately seven hundred mostly combat-related injured soldiers, and about a hundred of which were mental problems that they claimed was caused by curses put on them by witches working with the rebel forces. There were always other soldiers that claimed other physical problems such as blindness, deafness, and tumors that were put on them by witches working with the rebels. Albert would pray for them and I saw many healed of these curses or combat-related injuries.

Dr. Miguel Peñaloza

Albert W Luepnitz, international lecturer and evangelist, has been in close relationship with me for about five years, both in Colombia and the United States. I realize how much he loves

Colombia, and I have been a witness to his ministry of healing, all to the glory of God.

Albert mentioned to me about a problem of US Army and US Border Patrol Agents committing suicide. Albert could see a corresponding or similarity of this problem he encountered when ministering to Colombian soldiers and the ability of witches used by the drug cartel and rebel forces in Colombia to put curses of mental problems and suicide on these soldiers. I am from Colombia and can attest that Albert is correct.

However, this is a subject that we don't talk about in Colombia, and it would be doubtful if any Colombian government or military official would publicly acknowledge that this problem exists.

Fanny de Peñaloza

I want to express my gratitude for your prayers and love with us. Thousands of thanks because your prayer brought health to me after being so sick for this last year. I thank *God* because He used you in healing me. Glory be to our Lord!

Medellin, Colombia

About 1989 I was the designated speaker the following day at a Full Gospel Businessmen's Fellowship International meeting in Medellin, Colombia. I was at the Club Military in Bogotá when I received a telephone call from my interpreter in Medellin who had worked with me several times in that city. She said that she was told to tell me that if I attended the meeting tomorrow, the guerrillas will kill me.

I told her to tell them about Psalms 91:15-16: "*He shall call upon Me and I will answer him; I will be with him in trouble; I will deliver him and honor him*" (NKJV). I told her I would not only be in Medellin but that if they even touched me God would kill them. Arriving in Medellin the following afternoon I was taken directly to a large outdoor stadium. There were around eight thousand people in the stands and about four hundred in the playing field on stretchers and wheelchairs. My interpreter said there was a doctor and ambulance standing by in case I was shot. She stayed about ten feet from me.

I gave a message for about ten minutes addressing the threat but also gave a testimony. I suddenly commanded: "In the name of Jesus, I bind every spirit of darkness in this stadium and in the name of Jesus, come out." A person behind me who was holding a gun dropped it. Many in the stands and playing field started being delivered of demons. I continued to tell demons to come out in the name of Jesus. In a few minutes, I waved my hand toward the playing field and commanded: "Be healed in the name of Jesus." And everyone came out of wheelchairs and off of stretchers and started walking, running, and shouting.

Years later, I learned from a Colombian Army general that he was present at that meeting as a young officer but dressed as a civilian and that the commander of the FARC guerrillas was also there and received a healing. This probably gave me freedom to minister.

I am sure this got the attention of the guerrillas. I know it got mine. From that day on, even though I was ministering many times a few blocks of the drug cartel offices in Medellin, I was never threatened or bothered again.

I often gave a message on Medellin television and radio stations. On one occasion, I received a request to go to the terminal ill ward at a local hospital. Colonel Cifuentes was with me. The doctor asked me to pray for a thirteen-year-old girl who was in a coma for three months with very high blood pressure that was destroying her kidneys. They could not find an explanation for it. She was dying.

The Lord showed me where the blockage was that was causing the high blood pressure; I rebuked the problem in the name of Jesus, spoke healing, and commanded the high blood pressure to recede to normal in the name of Jesus. In about fifteen minutes, the blood pressure was normal and she awoke. She did have some kidney failure, and later I prayed for her and her kidneys were healed.

Over the years, I prayed for and saw thousands of individuals healed and accept Jesus in the Medellin area. On one occasion a woman in a wheelchair, pregnant, blind, and dying from a brain tumor was totally healed in the name of Jesus and later gave birth to a healthy baby girl. However, some were not healed.

About mid-1984 at a Full Gospel Businessmen's Fellowship International meeting in Medellin, Colombia, the then drug capital of the world and headquarters of the FARC guerrilla organization, there was a very large audience for a healing service. The ushers told me there were many guerrillas in the meeting and they all had concealed weapons. Their concern was that the meeting would end up with me and others being killed. I told them, "Well, I have them right where I want them." I don't recall what I spoke on, but one thing was for sure: the presence of the Holy Spirit was at a very high level and I knew it. Individuals with serious, terminal illnesses had been brought in ambulances to the meeting from local hospitals. Many that I prayed for were healed, but the highlight of the meeting was that many also went through a loud, screaming, extremely vigorous deliverance, expelling large amounts of black-looking mucus. I think the ushers locked the exit door as it seemed none were able to flee. Many were on the floor, crawling and screaming as I walked around, speaking, "Come out in the name of Jesus." When things finally settled down, I noticed that those that had been brought to the meeting in ambulances, on stretchers, were now walking. The guerrillas, when able to get up off the floor, fled the building.

The following evening, at the same meeting location, a

number of the hospital terminal patients shared how the doctors had already verified they were healed. There did not appear to be any guerrillas at this meeting.

I previously wrote about a time when Colonel Cifuentes and I prayed for a girl supposedly dying from terminally high blood pressure at a hospital in Medellin. She was healed. When we were leaving the hospital, we had to walk past about one hundred people that were standing and sitting in a hallway waiting to see a doctor. Most had been there for hours. We decided to pray for them. Colonel Cifuentes talked to several who were at the front of the line – all wanted prayer. It took us about thirty minutes to pray for all of them, one at a time. I would have loved to have seen what happened after we left. Later someone discovered no one was left in the hallway.

> *By faith Albert confronted the FARC*
> *guerrillas in Jesus' name – no weapon*
> *formed against him could prosper.*

Examples of the Glory of God

I accepted the fact that the presence of God was in all my meetings throughout North and South America. His presence through the authority in the name of Jesus and the power of the Holy Spirit was the only reason individuals received miracle healings and accepted Jesus Christ as their Savior.

However, in some meetings it was obvious that *His* presence was extraordinary as His display of power and signs excelled in every area of ministry. These are the testimonies I recall.

On the evening of February 6, 2009, I had just returned to Bogotá, Colombia, from meetings elsewhere in the country. A retired Colombian officer and a woman from the Full Gospel Businessmen's Fellowship International told me, "Albert, you are wanted at a Catholic church. We need to leave right now." The church was packed with hundreds of individuals rejoicing in singing. I was briefed by the presiding priest that it was a celebration for twenty newly graduated priests and all of them wanted me to lead them in receiving the baptism of the Holy Spirit. I had previously led many priests into this experience.

After the presiding priest addressed the new priests with a message, he had me come up on the platform with him. He introduced me and had the twenty line up in front. It was then that the priest told me we were on national TV and that millions of Spanish-speaking people, including Catholics in Central and South America would be watching this historic event, a first-time occurrence. I gave a message on salvation and then had these priests repeat a prayer of request, asking the Lord for the baptism of the Holy Spirit. As I placed my hand on the head of each one, I said, "Receive the Holy Spirit." And they would fall to the floor with an assistant catching them. As they came back on their feet, they all vocalized loudly their new heavenly language. We all cried with happiness and took many photographs. Because this service was on national TV, thousands of priests and lay people who were watching and participating in the prayer also received the baptism of the Holy Spirit

Another time, I was the guest speaker at a Full Gospel Businessmen's Fellowship International convention in Bogotá, Colombia, being held on a military base. I was just introduced for the Saturday evening healing service when people that were arriving entered the building, all very excited. My interpreter told me they were saying that a rainbow was wrapped around the building and they had to walk through it to enter!

I had been the guest speaker at these convention meetings for many years. There would always be many mothers or dads sitting on a row of chairs, holding their children that couldn't walk. I was always surprised for many different reasons, but one in particular was the number of children born with one or both hip sockets missing. When I placed my hand over their hips and spoke healing in the name of Jesus, they would be healed quicker than you could blink your eye. Not all, but most, were healed of whatever the problem was. I couldn't help but think, *Lord, how do you do that?*

For many years at all meetings throughout Colombia, I prayed for thousands of women with breast tumors, usually on the lower part of their breast, and most were healed. However, I wondered about this and started asking the brand name of their support bra. Almost everyone with tumors on the lower breast wore the same brand bra. I reported this to the Colombian government and this bra was pulled off the market. Within months, there would be very few breast tumor cases.

Once when I got off the plane in Bogotá, Colonel George took me straight to a hospital. A friend of his was in an accident; a large truck hit his car broadside and crushed it against a building. His friend was in the hospital and was not expected to live. While there, a doctor advised me that the injured man's muscles had been ripped off his ribs, causing a malfunction of the diaphragm muscle that controlled his lungs and they were not able to reattach them. He was also in a coma from a head injury and blunt trauma over most of his body. I took authority over the muscles and commanded in the name of Jesus they be reattached. I left the hospital as I had other meetings to attend. Later that afternoon, I received notice that the muscles had, in fact, reattached and he was now breathing normally. However, the pressure in his head was critical and I was asked to return to the hospital. I placed my hand on his head, spoke healing in the name of Jesus, and commanded the high pressure to cease and recede to normal. After a few minutes, he awaked from the coma and the doctor verified that the pressure was no longer a problem. However, he had sustained so many injuries that it took quite some time before he fully recovered.

Also, something very unusual happened at a military base somewhere near Bogotá, Colombia. Colonel George had driven for about an hour and there were about three hundred soldiers plus a lot of their dependents waiting at an outdoor field. A Catholic priest was giving a message, but stopped upon my arrival. I was introduced to the base commander, and he asked me if I would pray for each of them. The soldiers formed in a long line, side by side. I was limited on time so decided to just touch them and say, "In the name of Jesus be healed." The way I was walking along the line I did not notice what was happening behind me. At the end of the line, I looked back and all these soldiers were lying on their back on the ground, including the base commander. Even I was getting concerned as they stayed on the ground for some time. The priest excused himself and left. Everyone got up about the same time. The base commander and many of the soldiers expressed amazing stories of how they had received healing during the fifteen or twenty minutes they were on the ground.

In Bogotá, I was resting between meetings when a woman asked me if I could pray for her mother who lived nearby and was bed ridden. I went with her but didn't see any difference in her mother after prayer. The woman commented that her dad did not believe in God. So I decided to go fishing so I could reel him in. I asked the daughter if she had any health issues. She said that one leg was three inches shorter than the other. I set her on a chair, checked her legs, and asked her father to watch. When he saw the short leg grow even with the other, he set in the chair and he too had a short leg that grew. Then he asked me to pray for his eyes. I did and he got very excited when he discovered he was healed of color blindness. I reeled him in for Jesus, a big catch. We went to a very little restaurant he owned. We enjoyed a meal plus prayed for all his hired help. More good fishing.

By faith Albert went fishing.

****

Years ago in Saltillo, Mexico, I was visiting my brother Carl at his Christian Center. We received word of a young girl, apparently a relative of someone Carl knew, that was in the hospital dying of a very contagious disease. We went to the hospital and were told no one could go into the room as her disease was very contagious. When no one was looking, I slipped on a mask that was handy, entered the room, and prayed for her. Later the doctor was very puzzled when it was discovered she was healed. Carl could not believe what I did. I agreed and I wouldn't recommend doing this to anyone.

God Speaks Concerning Colombia

In the year 2005, I recently returned home from Colombia when I heard the following: "You have to return to Colombia. You are to establish intercessory prayer groups throughout Colombia for peace in Colombia and the reelection of the president." With the assistance of Colonel Cifuentes, National President of the Colombian Full Gospel Businessmen's Fellowship International, over a period of about one month, I went to eleven cities. I addressed many individuals in these cities and obtained promises of prayer about this subject. Many also were prayed over for health issues and received healing.

I returned to Bogotá on a Wednesday and heard the Lord say I was to see the president of Colombia, Alvaro Uribe Velez. However, no one seemed to be able to make such an appointment. I went to bed that night and made a comment, "Lord, if you want me to see the president, you will have to tell him. I don't know how." The following morning Colonel Cifuentes was notified that the president wanted to see me immediately. President Uribe asked me why I needed to see him. I told him what the Lord said about the prayer concerns and his re-election. He said, "Albert, I cannot be reelected because of term limitation." I said, "Mr. President, this says the Lord, 'You will be reelected' and the Lord will change the constitution to allow a second term." The constitution was changed and President Uribe was reelected. During his next term, the FARC organization suffered major losses and an additional one third of the country was recaptured. The change to the constitution was also for all future presidents.

President Uribe of Colombia thanking Albert for
his ministry in Colombia, South America

*By faith Albert spoke and the constitution was
changed and President Uribe re-elected.*

Testimony of José Rafael Aguirre

W hen I became a union leader, supported by the communists, I ended up believing in their ideology that denies God's existence and I joined the cause of the guerrillas, which promotes helping the poor by overthrowing the government, defeating the army and with the wealth of the rich make rich the poor. I believed these false statements in the same way even Catholic priests believed in them, among whom was priest Camilo Torres.

I believed in the ideology of not believing in God because when I was fourteen years old all my savings of four years of work had been stolen from me. That day I complained to God, crying and demanding from him an answer as to why He had allowed people to rob me, even when I had the knowledge that a Guardian Angel was protecting me. Then in that intense pain and no answer from God, I told Him: "I need you no more; I will manage on my own." And I stopped going to mass. About a year later, the communist leaders spoke to me and told me that God did not exist, that the Bible was written by rich people in order to exploit the poor. From then on, I made my mind up to fight against those deceivers because I had been robbed for believing in them.

For twenty-five years, I told people that God did not exist

and made propaganda that the guerrillas were the ones telling the truth. This went on until my mother, who believed in God and constantly urged me not to be stubborn, was run over by a vehicle and died. The next day at the funeral in the Catholic Church in the middle of Gregorian chants and the silence of the people, I remembered the words my mother said to me: "God does exist. Stop being stubborn. Believe in Him. I always pray for you and ask God for His protection upon you." And then I remembered the words I said to her during our last conversation: "God does not exist, Mother. Do not waste your time praying for me." Reliving this conversation, I cried out with all my strength: "God, if you really exist, give me my mother's faith!" I did this while pointing at my mother's coffin. People around me left their seats to hug me and calm me down, for they were surprised I was screaming to God like a crazy person.

From church, we headed out to the cemetery to bury my mother, and I kept asking myself if there really there is a God as my mother used to say. All week long, I kept on thinking and asking this same question: *Is there truly a God?* On Sunday, a thought came to me: *To go back to church as homage to my mother.* That is how I began attending church again Sunday after Sunday in memory of my mother and in case God might exist.

About eight months later, one Sunday, in a Protestant church my wife had started attending some months before, I decided to do what the worship leader was asking us to do. I lifted my hands, closed my eyes to avoid any distraction and repeated the song that goes, "Renew me, Lord Jesus. I do not want to be the same, for everything within me needs to be changed." I felt something special in my heart, like my heart getting warm and I started crying profusely. That was the precious day when Jesus Christ entered my heart because I asked Him: "Renew me, Lord. I do not want to be the same." From that day on, I paid more attention to the Word of God that is taught in church and I started understanding it. The hatred I felt towards the government and the army started disappearing and I even got invited to the Military Club for a meeting of the Full Gospel Businessmen's Fellowship International led by Colonel Armando Cifuentes. During the dinner, people shared their testimonies of how their lives had been transformed by the Lord Jesus Christ. It was in one of these meetings that I met a retired US military member. His name was Albert Luepnitz.

God started showing me His power through Albert, when he prayed in the name of Jesus Christ for a woman, an accountant by profession, who was crippled and whose body could not straighten up. I remember when Albert gave an order in the name of Jesus Christ and by the power of the Holy Spirit that each part of her paralyzed body be reestablished to its original state. I saw when miraculously her body came back to normal; she got up from her chair and started walking in that room, crying and glorifying God with great joy. Her name is Patricia Godoy. I will never forget this amazing miracle. From this miracle, my faith grew in God and I started reading more of the Bible. When I read in the Bible in 2 Timothy 3:16 that *"All Scripture is given by inspiration of God, and is profitable for doctrine, for reproof, for correction, for instruction in righteousness"* (NKJV), I realized I had a lot to correct in my life.

After this event at the Military Club, in which many people were healed from diverse illnesses, Albert and I traveled to different towns, doing the same that was done in Bogotá: healing the sick, pulling people out from darkness with the Word of God, and bringing the peace of Jesus Christ, which is different than the peace men give. I also had the chance to take Bibles to the demilitarized zone in the Colombian jungle (Caguan), which were disguised with a non-Bible cover, to give away to the guerrillas.

More Testimonies

Ayda Patrica Godoy

On February 26, 1986, I went to the Social Security Institute clinic for an examination of my uterus. The doctor ordered an anesthetic for me. While examining me, he realized the severity of my situation and decided to remove an ovary and fallopian tube. He also gave me another dose of anesthesia. This caused a total loss of sensitivity and my vital signs did not respond to the stimulator or cardiac resuscitator. The doctor declared I was dead. I felt alive and could hear everything, including doctors giving orders to move my body to the morgue. Then I was placed in a refrigerator for fourteen hours. My spirit was out of my body and I realized what they were doing. I saw my body and wondered what happened to me. My desire to live was huge and I was saying I was not dead because I could see myself. Suddenly my spirit floated in a brightly lit tunnel. There I experienced so much peace and tranquility; all was harmony. The more I advanced the darker it was in the tunnel. Reaching the end of the tunnel, I heard a heavenly voice saying, "Not yet." I understood that God had revived me and sent my spirit back to my body. At 4:30 a.m., I woke up in the freezing morgue and started yelling. The guard shouted, "The dead has awakened," and he ran through the clinic. The nurses ordered me to get up but I kept falling. At 7:00 a.m., the doctors decided to send me home. The Social Security Institute ordered a series of tests. They determined I could not walk.

On Holy Saturday in 1988, a sister invited me to a healing service given by Albert Luepnitz at a meeting of the Full Gospel Businessmen's Fellowship International. It had been two and a half years, and I had seen many doctors and no longer nourished any hope of walking again. I went to the meeting and was crawling and full of distress because they were about to close the door. I was the last one to enter. To my surprise, I recognized the doctor that worked at the clinic and knew my situation. He was Albert's interpreter. I was placed in the front row and Albert said, "The last shall be first." Albert placed his fingers in my ear as I had internal labyrinth destruction in my left ear because of the double dose of anesthesia, which affected my ability to walk.

Albert prayed for me and ordered me to jump. I started walking. The Lord totally healed me. He also prayed for my son who had suffered from reflux and he too was healed. Kneeling, I thanked God for my healing.

Colonel Armando Cifuentes Espinosa, Bogotá, Colombia

One of the persons who have greatly influenced the plan of God throughout Colombia is Mr. Albert Luepnitz. For over twenty-five years, Albert has been visiting, counseling and helping those in need due to illness, injuries, broken homes, alcoholism, and drug addiction. He has been a great blessing for all those who know him, engaged in a special task that has led to his recognition by the Colombian people throughout the country.

He has visited many military units: brigades, battalions, some on top of high mountains, where he prayed for diseased people and other personal needs, giving the soldiers courage in a mission that they are fulfilling and is empowering their faith.

It should be noted that this important work has a very sufficient impact on the health of the Colombian Army. When he prayed for these soldiers who were sick or injured as a result of confrontation with the guerrillas, rebels, and crime in general, many received miracle healings. This led many to believe in the power of God and His protection.

Today, with the deviating modernism and lack of spiritual life, I highly recommend that any nation get to know Albert and to use him in these very important activities that help many people in all their needs.

Angela Aquirre
September 28, 2010
I was told by Jaimie and my dad to write about the things I have seen when I ministered in Bogotá.

The times I translated for Albert Luepnitz in Bogotá have been opportunities to see God's wonderful power at work. I remember seeing ladies suffering from cysts and tumors asking God for healing. Albert asked them if they could feel the tumors with their hands and then asked them to place their hands on the tumor while he was rebuking the tumor in Jesus' name. Then, after checking the tumor, I remember seeing their faces in astonishment, it was gone. The reaction is like, "Please pray for this malady to go away," and when healing comes, it is almost unbelievable.

Of the various miracles God has performed, using Albert, one that still amazes me is of a little child. His mother was concerned, because the child had growth problems; he was too short for his age. She asked Albert to pray for her son that God would help him grow.

Albert asked this mother to bring the child to him. With

the child standing up in front of him, Albert asked the mother the height she would like for her son. He lifted his hand and asked this much. Finally, the mother showed how much. Then Albert prayed to God for the kid to grow and what happened still blows my mind. The child grew up to the height he was prayed for. It was as if the child was stretching from toe to head! I had never heard or seen anything like it before. And even if I had been told about this miracle, I would doubt it. But since I was standing with Albert to translate, I witnessed with my own eyes this miracle. It amazes me, the power of God. It is a huge miracle, for just in seconds the tissues, bones, muscles were all growing together in the name of Jesus Christ, the Creator of everything.

Liliana Castellanos Vivas

I met Albert Luepnitz in May 2004, when the Full Gospel Businessmen's Fellowship International requested my help to contact him via e-mail and organize his coming to Colombia. Thus began a relationship of very nice friendship that has lasted to this day. These various meetings lasted for one month and I was his translator.

We had prayers of all kinds with healings of diseases, tumors in the ovaries, breasts, someone with an enlarged prostate, and colon problems. Many with one leg shorter than the other grew to the same size in about thirty seconds. In all these prayers, Albert had absolute faith that God was going to do a miracle. He always started praying for cysts and tumors and asked the person to touch it as he was praying until it disappeared. It was incredible, really amazing, to see the power of God manifested as well. One of the greatest miracles took place at the Convention in June 2004. A woman who had been paralyzed five years from a drug that had poisoned her was totally healed when Albert prayed for her.

Albert came at least once a year to the conventions and always saw many miracle healings, with demonstrations of power of the Holy Spirit in healing all sorts of diseases, with all glory to God. In these meetings and others throughout the year, Albert prayed for and saw missing hip bones created, people with growth problems to grow taller, some several feet with even their clothing increasing in size as they grew. People with umbilical hernias felt them disappear when Albert prayed for them. At meetings on the military bases, there were soldiers wounded from combat injuries, Albert prayed for many that were blind and deaf and they were healed.

In 2005, we were on a farm praying for a family. It was here that I received, through the prayer of Albert, the gift of speaking in tongues. At this farm, Albert prayed for a man who for months had been connected to a bag to be able to urinate because of a witchcraft curse. The doctors were unable to conduct surgery to correct the problem because of the location of the obstruction and he was facing the risk of becoming impotent. He was not only healed but later had a son.

Albert is a man who has ministered with such passion. God has used him for all kinds of miracle healings and his ministry has increased.

By faith many were introduced to
divine encounters by Albert.

God Speaks to Albert

During the Christmas holidays in December 2008, at about 2 a.m. in the morning, I was sitting in my easy chair, crying. My dog, Pearl, was on my lap and whining (she's a very sensitive dog). I guess she was grieving like I was over the death of my wife a few months previously.

Suddenly, I heard someone speaking to me that I immediately recognized had to be Jesus. He said, "Albert, I am the One that calms the sea. Release that grief in you to me, for I am the one who will heal thee." I thought, *why didn't I think of that?* And did so. I felt at peace and stopped crying. Then He said, "I want all of you. I am increasing your anointing and your meetings in Colombia." That was it – no further message.

Later that day I telephoned a friend, but did not mention the message. We talked about some things and suddenly he said, "Al, the Lord told me to tell you He wants all of you." I thought about what I was not doing.

In January 2009, I went to Bogotá, Colombia, as I was the guest speaker at a Full Gospel Businessmen's Fellowship International meeting. Prior to the meeting, a woman named Marie, who is a prophet, talked to me and told me exactly what the Lord said. Now I was getting nervous about the "I want all of you."

At the meeting, I was introduced by Colonel Cifuentes. I

gave a short message and testimony. When I was ready to pray for people a woman came up holding a small baby. She said, "Albert, this child is three years old and has never grown." What happened next amazed me: As I held him, he started growing. I stood him on the floor and within a couple of minutes; he had grown to a full-sized three-year-old. Even his diaper grew. A Colombian woman named Angela was my interpreter. Many women with breast tumors were also healed.

At a later date, I was ministering in Armenia, Colombia. Several children with growth issues, undersize for their age, with a parent present and determining the height desired by placing their hand above the child. I commanded in the name of Jesus and they all grew to the desired height. A medical doctor was my interpreter. These were not midgets.

These events started a completely new area of creative miracles. It was also the beginning of seeing an increase in the healing of many children born with missing hip sockets.

By faith the child grew to his desired height.

"I Want All of You"

In December 2008, when the Lord told me he wanted all of me, I was very concerned. *What is He telling me? What have I not been doing?* It took a long time to find out.

Just recently, He finally gave me a clear vision of what He means. In 1981, He told me twice: "I have trained you in many things. I have made you financially secure. I want you to help the needy and the poor, to spread the gospel of Jesus Christ and to work for *Me*." In subsequent years, I diligently ministered throughout North and South America, even in some areas where many other ministers were killed.

In November 2014, I was meditating about this when I saw, a vision in large print, TO WORK FOR ME. The Lord asked me something: "Do you understand what I meant to work for me? You were not assigned by a church to serve me like most other envoys or personal desire, but I called you to be '*my* ambassador.'"

Many times during my loneliness while at home I thought about how nice it would be to again have a wife. My wife Joyce had died six years earlier. We all have a desire for a deep soul relationship with another, to be loved exclusively. But the Lord was teaching me something. I have to be satisfied, fulfilled, and content with being loved by *Him*, giving myself totally and unreservedly to *Him*, to have an intensely personal and unique relationship with *Him*, discovering that I must be united to *Him*, exclusive of anyone or anything else, exclusive of any other desires or longings.

The Lord said, "You must keep seeking *Me*, experiencing satisfaction, listening, and learning things I tell you. Don't be anxious. Don't worry. Don't look around you at what you think you want or you will sometimes miss what I want to do through you. In December 2008, when you were ready, I surprised you with an increase of *My* love far more wonderful than you could ever dream of. But until you are both satisfied exclusively with *Me* and the life I have given you, you won't be able to experience all the love that exemplifies your relationship with *Me* and thus the perfect love. Know that I love literally. Believe it and be satisfied."

The result of this has been the ability to go from less of me, to none of me, to all of *Him* the best I know how with *His* help. Total surrender to the Lord with no compromise, divesting myself of every encumbrance and hindrance the best I can, to become all that *His* Word says we are, results in total transformation.

By faith Albert, surprised with such an increase of
God's love, is called to embrace a total surrender.

Russell Stendal and Alethia

In 2009, I was ministering in Bogotá, Colombia, when I received an invitation to speak to a group of high-ranking Colombian military officers. The invitation came from Colonel Armando Cifuentes Espinosa, a military intelligence officer, president of the Full Gospel Businessmen's Fellowship International, and someone I had been ministering with for several years. Even the commanding general of the Colombian Army attended the luncheon. While there, I spoke about the prophecy the Lord gave me that changed the constitution of Colombia to allow the president a second term in office as well as several other issues. I happened to notice a young lady taking photographs of the meeting. It was obvious that she had a back problem. Her father, a gentleman named Russell Stendal, served as my Spanish-language interpreter for the gathering.

Following the meeting, I spoke to the young woman, Alethia Stendal, and offered to pray for her. As a result of the prayer, she was healed of a deformed back problem that she had been self-conscious of most of her young life.

A few months later, I again met Russell and Alethia when I was ministering on a military base in Bogotá. They had a woman with them named Joana who, they explain, had an incurable back condition. Joana had one leg substantially shorter than the other, plus a disk and muscle disease for which several doctors had told her there was no cure. When I prayed for her, the short leg grew and her back was totally healed in just a few minutes.

A few days later, Russell asked me to minister at his facility where he made CD recordings with messages to be transmitted to the FARC guerrilla organization. One example is of a little girl who regained her ability to talk, having not spoken for a number of years since her father was killed right in front of her by the guerrillas. A young woman with Down's syndrome was also healed and the change in her appearance was total and immediate. About thirty others were also healed. Russell was very impressed with the way I handled the meeting, which was just a quiet healing service with all the glory going to God.

During the following years, I had many ministry meetings throughout Colombia, arranged by Russell and or Alethia with perhaps thousands of miracle healings and decisions for Christ. All of Russell's family were healed of something when I prayed for them. Two of Russell's grandchildren were healed of severe back problems and each had one leg over three inches shorter than the other that grew to the same length. Some individuals that had serious eye problems, even blindness, were mostly all healed during meetings at Russell's home. At one meeting in a southern town, a daughter and her mother, each born with only one breast, received a second breast.

I was with Russell at a number of meetings with the Colombian Indian tribes. In the last meeting, I prayed for over fifteen hundred Indians. Over thirty of them, who were completely or legally blind, regained their sight, plus many others received a miraculous touch for various health problems, such as hernias, back problems, cancer, and about anything one could have.

Testimony by Alethia

May 26, 2010

My whole life, my mom, grandma, and others would criticize me for walking with a slouch. I thought it was just a bad habit until six months ago when my dad invited me to come with him and take pictures at an officer's breakfast meeting on the military base.

At the breakfast, a man named Albert, whom I had never met before, spoke of how four years ago the Lord had told him to tell President Uribe that he would be reelected and sure enough he was. He also told of all the healings he had witnessed in Colombia, especially in the army: deaf and blind soldiers being healed and twisted limbs growing, etc. My dad translated. After the meeting while I was busy taking pictures, out of the blue, Albert came up to me and said, "Do you have a back problem?" I thought, *no*. I hope he hadn't noticed my slouch. How embarrassing. My first reply was, "No, not that I can think of." But then I remembered all the things my mom would say. So I said he could pray for me if he wanted.

He sat me on a chair with my back centered and measured my two legs and sure enough, one was longer than the other by about an inch. I saw my leg grow miraculously by the hand of the Lord. And then Albert had me stand up and he checked my back and saw that my spinal cord was crooked. He said, "You feel this here? It's twisted." So he prayed a short prayer and the Lord completely straightened my back. It felt as if a gentle hand had softly straightened it, kind of like when you straighten out one of your fingers after clenching them in a fist. I felt no pain or anything like when you go to a chiropractor. The one thing I learned is that no matter how crooked you are, it is impossible for you to straighten yourself out. The only one who can straighten you is God, both spiritually and naturally … and sometimes (like in my case) you don't even know that you need to be straightened. Albert says that the name of Jesus has power over the flesh.

I went to Canada and North America, spoke at several places and when I came back to Colombia, I found that I had a new roommate. Her name was Joana and she belonged to the FARC guerrilla movement in Columbia. Our suspicion was that they sent her to spy on us under the pretext that she was "sick." When she got here, it turned out that she really was sick. We took her to several different doctors. They gave her tests and found out that her spinal cord was severely deteriorated and all the muscles in her back were completely damaged. In one accord, all the doctors decided that she was never going to get better. They said she had no hope and the only thing they could do about her problem was to teach her how to do back therapies. They said that no matter what she did, she would always be in pain for the rest of her life. Joana was very, very devastated when she heard this. She had been sick for twelve years. That day she cried. But she started going to muscle therapy twice a week and learned well. However, every night she would complain to me about how everything hurt.

She stayed with us for three months and in those three months, I saw her heart soften. One day I found her crying in the living room. When I asked her what was wrong, she told me that she missed her mom. I really wasn't expecting that answer coming from a tough guerrilla girl. So I told her we would make arrangements for her to see her mom and sure enough, a week later her Christian mom and grandmother, whom she had not seen since she ran away from home fourteen years ago, came to see her. They had been praying for her ever since.

One day she told my mom and me that the way we talked about God was admirable. She said we talked about Him as if we really knew Him and she wanted to know how she could have that relationship too. We definitely saw the hand of the Lord working on her. We saw her heart change. Of all the guests we'd ever had from Colombia and elsewhere, I told my dad that she was by far the one with the most hunger and longing and a docile heart for God.

A few days before she had to leave for the jungle, my dad called me in the room and told me that Albert was here again and he wanted to take Joana to see him. My mom and I talked with her in the living room and I told her how the Lord had healed me and how if she had even just a little faith, He could do it for her too. I gave her the option of going or staying. She listened intently and decided to go. We didn't tell her, however, that this man was waiting for us in a military base! My sister, my mom, my dad, Joana, and I hopped in the truck and drove down to the base. When she realized where we were taking her, she later told us that she almost had a heart attack. She was so scared. After all, these were the people she had fought against all her life. Here we were seeing armed camouflaged military personnel everywhere. I could just imagine what was going on in her mind. As we walked through the base, all I could do was laugh to myself because I thought that God really does have a sense of humor.

We all walked in the room where Albert was and he prayed for her. She had the same problem that I had where one leg was shorter than the other and we all saw it grow. And then she stood up and Albert prayed for her back and the hump that was there was completely straightened. She said afterward that she felt a hot tingling come over her whole body. She felt no pain from that point on. The Lord really healed her.

As we walked out, she told me that she was glad that she had her own experience with God because now she knew for sure that He existed and that He loved her. This happened on April 12, 2010, exactly six months after I was healed of a similar problem. To me this was significant because I realized that God didn't make exceptions of people no matter who they were or what they had done. Joana went back to the guerrillas a few days later. Her last words to my sister and me as she left were that she couldn't leave the movement because they'd kill her but now that she knew better she couldn't behave as bad as she had before. She asked us to pray for her freedom, because once you join the guerrillas, there is no way out unless you die or the Lord does a miracle. But we've witnessed time and time again that He is able to do anything. My sister and I will keep praying for her freedom and for others in there as well. We hope you join us.

During the same trip, Albert visited our congregation. Again, God did marvelous things through him. We knew of specific people who were suffering all kinds of problems. Some had heart problems; others had back pain, crippled limbs, or serious arthritis. There was a little girl who couldn't talk since she saw someone murder her father years ago. Albert sat her on his lap and began to sing "Jesus Loves Me" to her. My brother translated the words and soon she began to sing back and then she could talk! There was another girl with Down's syndrome who had deviated eyes. Her eyes and face became normal and she wandered around the room in awe without her thick glasses, seeing detail for the very first time. My mom and dad witnessed how the Lord healed more than thirty people. But the most important thing for everybody involved was to realize that the Lord was the one who was healing and nobody but Him got the credit. It was also a very respectful situation, not the screaming, hollering mess that has been seen in other "revivals." My mom told me that what she learned is that when you walk with the Lord, He gives you so much love, and the love of God will bring healing to the nations, whether it is physical healing or spiritual healing.

****

The day after Joana went back to the guerrillas (April 19), we were all very worried that government bombers would bomb her camp. That day we received the following e-mail:

> Sunrise in Whitehorse received your prayer alert and as I was praying for your people in Colombia and other places in South America I saw the following vision:

> "I saw bomber planes flying overhead. They were flying over the campfires where natives were dancing around the fires, doing a war dance. Then I saw white sheets cover some campfire scenes. The sheets represented the people totally surrendering to God. At some campfires there were no white sheets because those people were unable to surrender. The places that were surrendered were safe from the bomber planes; the planes simply looked and flew on by them. The places that did not surrender left themselves open for attacks from the planes."

Please continue to pray for Joana and for her commander, named Jorge, who has authorized his personnel to listen to our radio stations. Up until now, these guerrillas have been responsible for the murder of many pastors and for much persecution of evangelical Christians. Through the prayer and support of people like you, God has enabled us to keep all our radio stations on the air.

After many months, Albert came to visit us once again. Something special always happens on his visits. On this occasion, we were in Cali, Colombia, praying for all the Indians in that region. The Indian leaders had set up a day for Albert to speak and to pray for them. Bus after bus full of Indians filled the parking lot and the place was packed with about a thousand people. The leaders of that church service began to ask people for money, and for anything they had on: chains, watches, rings etc. When Albert got up to pray, my dad, Russell Stendal (a missionary to the Indian tribes in Colombia), introduced him by saying that what distinguished Albert from the rest of the people who had similar gifts like his is that he never charges a penny for using his gift to heal people. One by one, they came up and were healed of their various ailments. Albert visited three different Indian groups and must have prayed for hundreds in that weekend alone. He was scheduled to fly out on Thursday night from Cali, but on Tuesday my hairdresser, Mirian, a sweet Christian friend, called and said that she had finally convinced her cousin's husband Carlos, an "atheist" who works for the president of Colombia, and has access to all the prisons in the country, to let us into the maximum security prison in Bogotá. I had told her about Albert and his healing ministry and she moved heaven and earth to get Carlos to let us into the prison. Albert had been praying for every single side of the conflict except the paramilitary and this prison was full of former paramilitary leaders who had surrendered after the true events of the film *La Montaña* were revealed. These were real characters portrayed in that movie, now doing their time in jail. When I heard that we finally had access to pray for these prisoners, I didn't hesitate to buy Albert and my dad tickets to leave Cali on Wednesday afternoon.

In Bogotá, I had a friend with back problems so I asked her to come over to be prayed for on Wednesday night. She said, "A girl I know is dying of leukemia. Can Albert pray for her too?" I asked Albert and he didn't hesitate for a second before saying, "Of course!" Then I called my hairdresser, Mirian, and asked her if she could come to the house to "cut my hair." She said yes. The truth is I didn't need a haircut. It was all a trick to get her over so that Albert could pray for her. I also told my cousin to come have "yogurt" at my house. And he also came. My hairdresser, in turn, brought her cousin's husband Carlos, the guy that was going to get us into the prison. Just like I tricked my hairdresser into coming to my house to "cut my hair," she tricked Carlos into coming, telling him she wanted to invite him out to "eat." She chose a restaurant near our house and before going to it, she said, "There is a missionary called Russell who lives just up this hill. Let me introduce you to him before we eat." So they came up the hill to our house and to her surprise, I was waiting for her with Albert and my parents.

Meanwhile, a sixteen-year-old girl who was dying of cancer was also at my house with her parents, her sisters, and grandmother. They had just gone to the hospital that day, only to be told the horrible news that there was no more hope. Her family was devastated. They came to our house at night and we held a small meeting there, along with the people who were "tricked" into coming: Mirian and her daughter, Carlos, and my cousin. Everyone was healed of something. I think the most spectacular healing that night was Mirian's who had one foot about two inches smaller than the other. Albert told me to get a pen to measure her toes and we marked a line through one foot to the next. He prayed and the shorter foot grew and became as big as the other one, the line I had drawn was now two inches uneven. When this miracle happened, everyone in the room started weeping. Mirian walked around, and in awe smiled, saying that her foot didn't hurt anymore. Albert spoke of forgiveness and how it was necessary to forgive our parents because in many cases they were also just victims of their own parents. He said that in order to receive God's blessing, it was necessary to "honor" our father and mother, "no matter what." When he spoke this, Mirian's daughter began to sob. She had an abusive father that had left them both when she was little and apparently, even now in her twenties, the hurts had not been healed yet. Then a woman who had problems with her eyesight came up and Albert prayed for her and when he was done she smiled and said that she could see perfectly and that her eyes didn't hurt anymore. About twelve people were prayed for in our small living room. The girl with leukemia was crying as she saw all the miracles happen before her eyes. It gave her hope that she could be healed too. Albert hugged her and prayed that her white blood cells would reproduce and that she would be healed. When he got done praying for her, she started crying and her father told us how they had been dealing with her leukemia ever since she was only six years old. They had spent the past two years in the hospital. We believe the Lord did heal her that night and we are expectantly waiting for the test results. That family left our apartment building with new hope. Albert told them to reject any death sentence that the doctors might have given them in the name of Jesus.

Earlier that day, Albert prayed for my four-year-old nephew who had one leg about three inches shorter than the other one. To his nanny's surprise, his leg grew to the length of the other one. Then Albert measured his feet and one foot was significantly shorter than the other one. It also grew. We looked at my little nephew and he was still walking a little funny so Albert checked his hips. When he prayed for them, something snapped and they got back in place. My nephew now has what he calls "Superman feet." His nanny was completely shocked when she saw all these miracles happen. This was all very new to her. Being a very shy person, she mustered the courage to ask Albert to pray for the tumors she had in her breasts. She had been dealing with this problem for years and going to the doctors every month just to get her breasts checked in case the problem developed into a cancerous tumor. Albert told her to put her hands where she could feel the tumors and he prayed for her. The tumors left immediately. She smiled and her eyes watered as she felt her breasts and could not find anything. Her mom was also healed of a terrible back problem she had had for years. And my mom's knee was prayed for. She had been having trouble with it for years and the cartilage in it was immediately restored when Albert prayed for her.

While these miracles were taking place, the very-hard-to-get Carlos, the presidential guy, was chatting away on his cell phone, not taking any notice of what was happening. As Mirian and Carlos were on their way out, my dad asked him if he wanted to be prayed for by Albert. Carlos nodded in a "get-me-out-of-here" way. But Albert sat him down on a chair, measured both legs, and noticed one was shorter than the other one. It grew. Then Albert prayed for his knee that was bent and it straightened out completely. When this happened, Carlos could not believe it. His eyes got really big and he said that the pain was gone and that he had felt a warm sensation on his knee while Albert was praying. I don't think he knew what had hit him. Then Albert told Carlos to stand at attention and his back, which had been hurt in a bomb blast, snapped perfectly back into place.

The next day Albert, my dad, and I went to meet up with Carlos in the maximum security prison. The prison was not as bad as I thought it would be, as it included a church, a garden, and a basketball/soccer court.

When the paramilitary men saw us come in, they all gathered in a small room to hear Albert and my dad speak. Albert told of his time in the army and how he could relate to their hard shell as a result. He said that in the army, a hard shell develops, and it is impossible to get rid of it without the power of the Lord Jesus Christ. Albert asked me to tell of some of the miracles I had seen that week, so I gave them a report on what had happened.

Surprisingly, Carlos spoke up and told the story of how the Lord healed him the day before. These seemingly tough guys eagerly lined up so Albert could pray for them. Then my dad led them in a powerful prayer, which they prayed fervently, "Lord, deliver me from my past, from the nightmares that haunt me. I give myself to You and only You."

They all repeated this prayer fervently. One of the main leaders was healed of multiple diseases. Another one was demon–possessed and Albert cast it out in the name of Jesus. Many legs and knees were healed and grew back to normal. Crossed eyes were made straight. In essence, those hard-shelled men became soft. We are happy to see how God is touching people on all sides to this seemingly never-ending war. Many prophets have come up to Albert to tell him that his time in Colombia is not over, and that God still needs him here for many more years to come. We hope this is the case.

> *By faith Albert listened, obeyed, and perse-*
> *vered, visiting often with the Stendal's heal-*
> *ing many, always in Jesus' name.*

A Miracle Healing that Could
Bring Peace to Colombia

———⎯⎯✧⎯⎯———

In January 2013, I was in Temple, Texas, visiting my brother when I received a telephone call from Russell Stendal, who I had ministered with for years in Colombia, South America. Russell said it was very urgent that I meet him at a missionary pilot training facility in Ironton, Missouri. He asked me to return to Longview, Texas, immediately and meet someone flying a private plane to get me.

When I met with Russell he told me he had an urgent mission to meet with several government officials in the country of Cuba. Russell told me it was a very important meeting and that he and others prayed about the mission to be accomplished and the Lord told them to use Albert. I have known Russell well enough that I would not doubt for a minute what he was asking of me, so I agreed.

In a few days, we were flying in a commercial plane from Panama City, Panama, to Havana, Cuba. I had a seat in first class and Russell and a doctor friend were in the back. About an hour into the flight, someone looking like a person was standing in the aisle looking at me. This figure was a white male, with long hair to his shoulders, no sign of even needing to shave and dressed in a white garment that reached to the floor. In a few minutes, I realized that this had to be my guardian angel. We looked at each other for at least five minutes and he just disappeared. I was so amazed I didn't even say anything. When I told Russell and the doctor, they were delighted; believing as I did it was a good indication our mission would be successful.

In Havana, we went through immigration and exited to the lobby area. An individual named Noel met us and seemed to know Russell. One other individual was with Noel. We got in a late model van with two Cuban men in the front. We checked into a very nice hotel which I understood was for tourists.

Russell explained to me that Noel and the other guy named Yuri were an advance party of leaders of the Colombian FARC'S guerrilla organization. Noel was the guerrilla that had helped arrange Russell's release in 1983 after he had been held prisoner for ransom for six months. The president of Colombia had asked the FARC to discuss a peace treaty. The Colombian government delegates and FARC leaders were to hold meetings in Cuba. The Colombian delegates would not arrive for several days and the FARC leaders in a couple of days.

Our mission: To encourage the FARC leadership delegates to agree to pursue a peace treaty. I had a couple of days to digest this predicament, as I was concerned about the controversial problem of getting involved.

I am very astute when ministering, hearing from the Lord for guidance, following His directions and suppression of negative thinking by taking every thought captive to the obedience of Christ (2 Corinthians 10:5). My ministering to the FARC was not to be with persuasive words of human wisdom, but in demonstration of the spirit and of power (1 Corinthians 2:4-5).

I accepted the fact that Russell had heard from the Lord that He was to use me. That being the case I accepted it, as a promise from God that if I did not waver through unbelief, but be strengthened in faith, giving glory to God the mission would be a success (Romans 4:20).My guardian angel was standing by. It would have been nice if he would have just given me a hug.

In a few days, the main FARC leadership arrived at the hotel with Ivan, the number two commander, a man named Santrich, who was blind, and a young woman named Maritza, who was Ivan's companion. We were well received. Maritza sat down and I could not help but notice her facial expression indicated extreme stress and pain.

The following evening Russell, the doctor and I were taken to the residence where the FARC delegation were staying. Ivan was in a private bedroom with Maritza.

The ones needing healing came into the room one at a time. Santrich was the first to be prayed for. Besides being blind he had been poisoned and the damage to his stomach left him only able to drink soup. He received healing for his stomach, but not for blindness.

Maritza said she had received injuries to her right foot and left shoulder from fragments of a mine she stepped on. She had healed but she was in extreme pain with obvious disfigurement. I asked Maritza to sit on a chair and place her injured foot on another chair in front of her. I placed my hand on her foot and spoke healing in the name of Jesus. Her foot was immediately transformed with no evidence of the injuries. Even a toe that was short since birth grew to normal length and the pain was gone. Ivan commented to Russell about some other powerful spirit I had. Russell corrected him: *"No, the healing is in the name of Jesus."* Ivan then also wanted prayer.

Exuberant joy was immediate. The change of facial expressions on these individuals was amazing. Everyone hugged me and took pictures, especially of Maritza with me.

On the outside I was smiling and on the inside was thinking, *My God, you sure gave this group a whole new application of who You are and that Your healing of Maritza was a turning point in their life, the beginning to full acceptance of Jesus.*

The second evening we had a dinner meeting with them. Ivan, with obvious tears, hugged me and said, "Thank you, thank you, Albert. Now we know that God loves us to. We have accepted Jesus and want to establish peace in Colombia." I thought I heard the Lord say, *"The miracle healing of Maritza will be a contributing factor for peace to Colombia."*

In April 2013, I was ministering in meetings in Vancouver, Canada. I was approached by an official who identified himself as being from the Colombian embassy in Canada. He wanted me to talk to the former president of Colombia, Alvado Uribe Velez, about a subject they suggested. I refused. I advised that the Lord had already told me what I had to do.

I was to return to Cuba and tell the Cuban delegation that the Lord told me that *"the peace treaty had to be done God's way, not man's way, or it would fail."* I returned to Cuba with Russell, his wife Marina, his daughter Alethia, and others. At a dinner meeting with Ivan, Santrich, and Maritza, I told them what the Lord demanded: "the killing on both sides had to stop; the peace treaty would only survive if it was done God's way, not man's way; the president should rally the women in Colombia to demand peace; if peace was not accomplished *His* way, there would be major consequences for Colombia."

I advised these FARC leaders that I did not come to meet them because I loved them, had not come because I hated them, but because the Lord told me to see them, so they better pay attention to what I was just conveying to them. I reminded them of the following verses of Scripture. I know what Jesus commanded us to do: *"Love your enemies and pray for those that persecute you, that you may be children of your Father in heaven"* (Matthew 5:43-45 NIV). Jesus also said, *"Blessed are the merciful, for they will be shown mercy. Blessed are the pure in heart, for they will see God. Blessed are the peacemakers, for they will be called children of God"* (Matthew 5: 7-9 NIV).

Our Cuban driver asked for prayer for his wife, who was in the hospital, experiencing a miscarriage at five months. She later told me, when I prayed for her, she actually felt the baby as it slid up into place and her womb closed.

When we returned to Bogotá and Russell arranged a meeting at his facility where he made CDs and had services. About fifty women were present and some men, including the Colombian president's cousin. I gave a detailed message on what the Lord required of the peace treaty with forgiveness on both sides necessary. I told about what the Lord said about the role of women that they wanted peace. The killing of their loved ones had to stop. Every woman in there stood up, clapped their hands, and agreed. I asked the president's cousin to convey to the president what he just saw and what the Lord demanded.

I later read on world news that is exactly what happened, including two women the president appointed to be with the Colombian peace delegation in Cuba.

During a previous visit to Cuba, my third trip, I had prayed for a FARC commander named Pablo Catattumbo, the one in charge of the FARC military operations. Pablo had a metal plate in his upper right arm and had very little use of his fingers. At that time, he was not healed.

On my last trip to Cuba in December 2014, I again prayed for Pablo. However, this time it was different as the Lord gave me direction. Pablo removed his shirt. I placed my left hand on his arm over the metal plate area and told him to grasp my right hand by squeezing with his fingers. I told him to squeeze every time I said "in the name of Jesus." At first, he showed no improvement but as I repeated "in the name of Jesus," I noticed an increase in pressure. After about twenty minutes, he was totally healed. I also prayed for the remaining FARC leaders I had not prayed for previously; all received healing. One asked permission to kiss me. He did, on my cheek and commented,

"I kiss you like I would my father, with love and thanks." They all said they wanted peace in Colombia.

These are the names of the FARC leadership I prayed for and saw healed: 1) the first ones, Ivan Marquez, Jesus Santrich, Maritiza; several lower ranks, 2) next in subsequent visits, Pablo Catatumbo, Romana, Pastor Alape, Freddy, Yuri, Noel and several names unknown; and 3) one who six months before had directed his troops to kill Russell. The one in the photo below fell off a cliff, fractured his back, but said he was healed when I prayed for him. The last I saw him he was hugging Russell. The woman in the photo below had received serious injuries to her stomach requiring several surgeries. She said she felt healed.

The president arranged for these FARC leaders to be confronted by many of their victims. Both sides did what the Lord told me in April 2013 to tell them, "Peace God's way, not man's way, accepting total forgiveness on both sides."

Russell and I both feel that now peace may finally be accomplished in Colombia after both of us dedicated over thirty-three years of our lives to the peace process.

By faith Albert believed for Maritza's miraculous divine encounter and opened the door to peace.

A Prophecy for Ivan Marquez

A word from the Lord Albert had for Ivan, head of the FARC peace delegation meeting in Cuba.

Ivan, on October 12, 2014 at 10:23 a.m., Albert had a word from the Lord for you:

> For almost two years, you have been on a detour of My purpose to use you in a way I cannot completely tell you unless you finish the detour and I can call you one of Mine.

> During this detour, I have shown you authority and power of the Holy Spirit through miracle healings and My Word, conveyed to you by My servants. I need your total submission to Me, says the Lord, so I can communicate with you like a son, to give you guidance and wisdom to accomplish and show you My way to peace in Colombia. You have to set aside your pre-conceived ideas so I can tell you, says the Lord.

> I cannot do this until you have shown you are one of Mine, says the Lord. Listen to My servants

whom I have sent you. They are My messengers.
Why are you holding back? Complete the detour.
Have I not demonstrated My love for you?

I asked Alethia if the Lord would confirm to her this message. Her reply: "I witness to this." I translated it and sent it to Ivan.

A prophesy for Ivan Marquez

I am sure by now that you realize that Russell and I are ambassadors of peace by direct assignment of our Lord and Savior, Jesus Christ. I, Albert, have been directed by the Lord to tell you the following. This says the Lord:

> "I want you to accept My invitation to be My witness of how much I love you, to convey to all concerned that you accepted Me and want peace in Colombia. I want you to acknowledge to the nation of Colombia that mistakes have been made by you and your organization and by both sides in this conflict. Tell them you have asked My forgiveness and then ask for their forgiveness. If you will, I want you to be a witness of the change in your life after you accepted Me, from the old man to the new. I want you to be very firm in the message that My direction is the only way to go in the peace process. The killing has to stop. There has to be complete and total unilateral forgiveness and the stopping of violence on both sides. Ivan, I want you as an example for all. My way is the only way for peace. You will be My witness as an example that only I, the Lord God, can make such a change in you and that I can do it for others and for a nation. I will guide you in such a spiritual way, to be witness of my love and direction, not only in

Colombia, but also to all other countries of South America."

On December 14, 2014, in a conversation with Ivan, Russell explained this to him and Ivan agreed to this prophecy.

By faith Albert prophesied and commissioned; and by faith Ivan received.

Front Row: Russell, Ivan, Maritza, Albert, and Santrich

A Story by Alethia Stendal

———⟨⟩———

Albert's visit to Colombia in January of 2014 came as a breath of fresh air. It didn't come as easy as I would have expected. He had written that he was scheduled to fly in on the 13th of January and stay until the 26th. I asked him if he could extend his trip a week and even though he had to pay an extra $300 airline penalty, he did. I told him that his money was well spent and he wouldn't regret it. Then I received an e-mail from him saying that he felt too tired and stressed out and that he thought it would be better if he stayed home and came another time. Although I admit I was a little disappointed, I told him to do whatever gave him peace. After about a week, he replied and said, "You know, I realize now, that ever since a year ago when I started going to Cuba and Colombia, the devil has always attacked me right before I leave, so I think this is another one of those attacks and I have decided to go."

We met at the airport on the morning of the 13th of January and flew to Neiva, a city in the southern part of the country. A distinguished Colombian lawyer who had been a senator and an advisor for many past presidents picked us up from the airport and invited us to his house for breakfast. On the drive there, the lawyer received a text saying that his mother had died. After twenty long minutes of uncertainty, he received another text from someone saying that it had been someone else's mother who died. I thought it might be a good time to ask him if he wanted Albert to pray for his mother. After thinking she was dead a few minutes ago, of course he was enthused about it and we went to her house. But first, Albert prayed for him. He had one leg shorter than the other and his back was twisted as a result. His leg grew out to the exact size as the other and his back was straightened. His mom, the cutest little old woman, was waiting for us when we got to her house. Everything that could be wrong with her was, Albert started with her arms. She couldn't move them anymore because the area beneath the two shoulders had caved in and formed two holes. Albert prayed and the caved in areas rose up again.

Alethia and Albert

With a twinkle in her eyes, she moved her arms up and down with no pain. Her heart and her lungs weren't functioning well because she had smoked when she was young and one finger had no movement due to an accident years earlier. This really inhibited her from sewing, her favorite hobby. Albert prayed for her in the name of Jesus and her finger was restored and immediately she began to breathe better. She had needed an oxygen mask before that. Little did we know that this little old woman would later be the key to the entrance of healing for the whole family and their friends. She had eight kids and it was obvious that all of them had so much respect for her as one by one they began flooding my cell phone with calls thanking us because "mom was very happy." Now they all wanted prayer. The lawyer told me that whenever we had a chance, he would pay for our tickets to come back and pray for the rest of his family.

We continued further south where we had other friends waiting for us. We had meetings in the towns of Garzón and La Plata. In our first meeting in Garzón, Albert began praying for every person there and after five minutes, he looked at me and said, "There's no anointing. What should we do?"

He kindly asked me to give a talk to the people so I addressed them and said, "Although seeing miracles is very nice, and it can awaken a lot of faith, it will never be His ultimate goal for us. When the Lord Jesus was here, what he longed for, more than any miracles, was for his disciples to know his Father so that they could discover His love and also be one with Him. There needs to be a complete surrender to God. What is the used of having your back healed if you don't know who He is? And when you let Him direct your life in every single detail, the big picture will turn out as it should. I learned this while making a movie: all I had to do was make sure every single detail was exactly where it needed to be to the best of my conscience, and the big picture came out exactly the way it was supposed to." Then Albert told some of the many stories where God had had a direct hand in his life. He began to pray for the people once again. Many of them were healed of different things like hernias, eye problems, legs and arms that were unequal and got evened out. A Jewish man said that although he wasn't the one who was being prayed for because he was at the other end of the room talking to a friend, all of a sudden felt a warmth come over his own spinal cord until it was completely restored. This happened while Albert was praying for someone else's back. His arm was also about three inches shorter than the other one and it grew to the length of the longer one!

I invited a Mormon friend of mine to the meeting because he had back problems. Albert measured his legs and that's where he found the cause of my friend Spencer's back problem; he had one leg about three inches shorter than the other one. Spencer felt his own leg grow to the same size as the other one. A few months earlier, Spencer's dad (a main leader in the Mormon Church), went through a difficult heart surgery and almost died. Since he had diabetes, he hadn't recovered fully and the doctors were contemplating re-operating on him. This was something that his dad and family obviously did not want to go through. So Spencer told his dad about what God had done for him and the next day he arrived with his dad at the house where we were staying. At first, Spencer's dad was very skeptical and was asking us a lot of questions like, "Who gave you the authority to heal people?" And Albert very humbly answered, "The Lord Jesus gave me the authority." Then the Mormon turned and asked me in Spanish, "But how do I know that he is genuine?" I said, "The Lord Jesus said that we shall know them by their fruits. Albert has been coming to Colombia for thirty years and has witnessed over one hundred thousand miracles here but he has never used his gifts of healing for his own personal gain. Every single trip has been spent with money from his own pocket and he never asks people to give him anything in exchange. That is something that is hard to find among people with God-given gifts." After asking a few more questions, he asked Albert to please pray for his heart. Albert prayed that the metal left from the surgery would disappear and that a full and complete healing would take place. This encounter opened the door into their whole family. That day we went to pray for their aunt and uncles, nieces, the grandma, the friends – everyone. God gave the Mormon family a tremendous blessing.

The next day we drove for an hour and a half for a meeting in a small, humble farm near the town of La Plata, an area known for having gone through a lot of violence and war in the past. They stood their ground when everything was against them, and putting their trust in God, He saw them through. Being faithful listeners of our radio station, they were anxiously awaiting one of the preachers that spoke on it: Albert. They served us a delicious, abundant lunch and then Albert took a nap in order to have strength for the meeting. After a quick twenty-minute snooze, we saw that people had all gathered in the garden and Albert began to pray for them one by one as

I translated. Everyone there was healed of something. Here is the report they sent me afterward:

A Testimony by Pabel

A very special greeting to everyone. May the Lord bless you all and I continually thank you for coming to this distant mountain in Huila bringing us the love of the Lord. We hope that the fullness of that love will germinate in every corner of our Colombia that you visit. May the Bright and Morning Star always guide your path.

Javier is a man who had a grave sickness where his defenses were always low; therefore, he could never work because he would have a crisis. But then he worked on his farm harvesting coffee and cutting grass the very next day without getting tired. His wife and his relatives are shocked and were telling him to get examined, but his wife told them no because it is the work of the Lord, and that made her happy. My daughter had been ordered a hip exam and now she doesn't need it, thanks to the Lord. I also had an unleveled hip and it would hurt when I would carry heavy items. And now I can carry a heavy load and nothing hurts. I also feel very light when I walk. I give thanks and honor to the Lord every day for healing me through the hand of Albert and Alethia.

Kelly had a deviated bone in her column that hurt her every time she sat down and now she is very thankful. My friend Jimeno also told me that he doesn't feel his hip is tired anymore and he's been working on construction these days. He gives many thanks to the Lord and Albert.

My son, Israel David, was also healed in his hip. Aguilar's arm suffered an accident and his arm would unlock from its socket every now and then, and now it doesn't. Blessed be the name of the Lord because great and marvelous are all His works.

God bless Brother Albert and Alethia and all their friends for remembering the weakest.

Davis now feels no pain in his back and he is very content.

Albert told them how he signed up with the army in World War II and served over twenty-four years. By 1979, his injuries caught up with him, resulting in being crippled with an incurable back problem, facing a life in a wheel chair. In 1981, a woman prayed for him and he received a miracle healing.

We love you and will always have you in our hearts.

– *Pabel*

(Note: Pabel was later murdered when caught donating Bibles to Indians. His wife, Kelly, forgave his murderers and asked that they not be punished. The Indian tribal leaders gave Kelly permission to distribute all the Bibles she wants without being bothered.)

Albert with Pabel and his son

Sonia, our neighbor, stopped suffering from the
extreme pain she had in her hip every day.

At our next meeting, a woman asked Albert to pray for her
baby's digestive track. Being a former detective for the US
Army, Albert began to drill her to find the real reason behind
her baby's problem. After many questions, he finally asked her
if she was breast-feeding the baby and she said no. "Why aren't
you breast-feeding your baby?" She smiled half-embarrassed
and said, "Sir, it's just that I only have one breast. The other
one is too small."

"Do you want me to pray that the smaller breast would grow
to the same size as the other one?"

With a bashful smile, the woman nodded in approval. She
put her hand over her non-existent breast and Albert put his
hand on her hand and prayed that it would grow to the same
size as the other. In just a second, the two breasts appeared to
be the same size. I saw the empty space in the shirt began to
press forward. It was amazing! Then Albert asked her if it ran

in the family, and she said that her mom also had that same problem. "Tell her to come here and let me pray for her," Albert said, as the mother of the woman shyly came up next to her daughter. In two seconds, the flat breast had grown to its full size. "See," he told them, "it is important to pray that this family line curse would be broken because it is possible that your little baby daughter could inherit the same problem."

That night the lawyer, whose mom we had prayed for on the first day, called asking if we could please pray for his 29-year-old nephew named German, who was dying of cancer. The next morning, we were on a plane to Bogotá. We arrived at a small two-bedroom apartment overlooking one of the main highways where German's dad was anxiously waiting for us with his sick son, his daughter, and two nurses. But before he prayed for German, Albert wanted the dad to see that the flesh responded to the name of Jesus. So he measured German's dad's legs, and one was shorter than the other one. In the name of Jesus, Albert prayed that the shorter one would grow to the same length as the other one. And it did. After a few more miracles with his daughter and the two nurses, Albert felt it was time to pray for cancer-stricken German. Albert laid his hand on the sick man's belly and immediately as he did this, strong anointing started flowing from his hand.

As he was praying for the young man, Albert took the opportunity to talk to the family and the nurses and tell them a little bit about what God had done in his life. He told them about how he had been in World War II. One time he was seriously injured and by 1980 had become completely handicapped. The doctors said he would most likely end up in a wheelchair the rest of his life, but his wife took him to a woman with the gift of healing and the woman said, "In the name of Jesus, be healed."

From that moment on, Albert was completely healed both emotionally and physically. Not only that, but he also received gifts of healing. After about twenty minutes of strong anointing, German fell into a deep sleep. He woke up after a few minutes and said he knew that God had a plan for his life and was using this illness to glorify Himself. I gave him a copy of the movie we made, *La Montaña*, and he immediately started watching it. The next day his dad called me and said that his son was at the mall with his friends!

The rest of the lawyer's extended family was so touched (and I guess sick as well) that they all drove a seven-hour trip to Bogotá just to have Albert pray for them. There was about ten of them that arrived at the house. One of them was a woman talking loudly on her cell phone the whole time Albert was trying to pray for people and he had to tell her to turn it off. When it came time for her turn for prayer, she asked that her eyes be prayed for. Before I had time to ask her what was wrong with her eyes, Albert began to see a vision of them, he said, "The Lord has just revealed to me that you see spots everywhere." I asked her if this was the case and she said yes. So, knowing exactly how to pray for her, Albert prayed that she might have a normal vision with no spots, and she did.

One memorable miracle was a man who had chest pain and didn't know why. When Albert prayed for him, he saw in a vision that one of his lungs was being obstructed, so again the

Lord showed him exactly how to pray. And the man began to breathe and feel completely fine. Another woman asked Albert to pray for her obesity and he said, "The only one who can do something about that is you." A woman with diabetes asked for prayer and Albert explained the difference between alkaline and acidic food and that people should eat more alkaline food than acidic if they want to avoid diabetes. Another woman's muscles ached tremendously and Albert told her that she had a magnesium deficiency and that she also needed more B6 and B12. This would help her muscles.

One of the things I learned is that although God can heal us of different things, the Lord doesn't do our homework for us. We have to be conscious of the fact that God did give us a brain and hopefully we will use our common sense and ask Him to show us how to be healthier. He may show you to not eat a certain thing because it is affecting your kidneys and He may show me something completely different. Although He can give us wisdom and discernment concerning our health, He does not intend for this to become an obsession to the point where we are completely focused on ourselves. He wants us to take the focus off of ourselves and onto Him. Too many people get sidetracked with themselves in diets, healthy precautions, such as "I don't eat this," "I don't eat that," "I just don't eat!" or "the doctor said this or that…" and what they are really doing is revolving their lives around the wrong thing and becoming completely powerless to do anything effective for God.

The next day we visited a woman who had been operated on for cancer four times in her throat. When Albert prayed for her, she started sweating and said she was hot all over. Albert said that it was the effects of the Holy Spirit working on her body. We conversed with her and her husband for a while until she said trivially, "I have anger issues that I am trying to resolve. I get upset at things really easily, and I don't know how to control it." Again, while using his detective skills, Albert said, "The mystery is solved! When you get angry, your stress goes up, and high stress is what causes your immune system to go down and it leaves the door open for any disease to come in. That is why you have had cancer four times."

So Albert explained about how his father had had rage problems and how it had passed on to his brother and it eventually killed him at a very young age. He said that the only way to break this curse, that unfortunately we all inherit as a result of the fall of mankind, is in the life of Jesus. When we live His life, instead of our own, we become a new creation, and that is when all things become new, even an inherited anger problem. However, there is price to pay: our own life, in exchange for His. Our own plans become submitted to His plans, and our desires become His desires because of the work He is doing in our hearts, for surely, He is the only one who can break any bondage we have inherited, with just one word.

That day the lawyer invited us out to lunch with his son and daughter who came with her husband and little baby. They took us to a nice Peruvian restaurant where we had delicious salmon and shrimp cocktail. The daughter asked me if Albert could pray for all of them. It was about 3 p.m. and we had another meeting at 4 p.m. We were in the middle of a restaurant with music playing. I said yes, but I told her that I didn't know where we could find the time or the space to do it, because supposedly Albert needed a quiet place to be able to hear God's voice correctly. We brainstormed the different options in Spanish, when Albert, who was talking to the lawyer's son, started saying, "Don't tell me what's wrong with you. I know exactly what is wrong with you because the Lord is giving me a vision of it right now. Your liver, your colon, and your kidneys are damaged because of all the alcohol you are consuming. They can't function properly anymore and that is what is causing the rash you have, your acne, and the diarrhea because the body needs to get the waste out somewhere. You are on the road to death and if you do not do something about it, you will be dead in a few years. I know you don't care much about your life, but what about the people you leave behind?"

His sister's jaw was wide open. She gave her brother a little shove and said, "See, I told you! You drink too much! I try telling him but he won't listen!" The next one Albert prayed for was her little baby daughter. She had one leg about three inches shorter than the other one and to the mother's amazement, the shorter leg grew just as big as the other one. Miracles seen in children always make the mothers cry. Next Albert prayed for her and her husband. By this time, a woman sitting at the table next to us saw everything and wanted Albert to pray for her too. So he prayed for her hip (which was dislocated) and we left as soon as we could before anyone else in the restaurant stopped us for prayer.

We arrived just in time for our meeting at 4:00 p.m. Albert gave a forty-minute talk for the radio station and must have prayed for a hundred people there. One family said that they didn't care if they got healed or not. What they really wanted was to have God's blessing and know that the Holy Spirit was with them. Albert prayed for their son and the mom cried as she saw her little son's leg grow about three inches. Many people were healed of various illnesses.

The next day we flew to another part of the country to pray for the Paez Indians. These fifty Christian families were displaced from their lands when a volcano destroyed everything, leaving them with nothing. The new land and homes that were supposed to come from the government were given to the tribal leaders who did not share with these families because they refused to renounce their Christian beliefs and follow the tribal rituals. See, years before, American missionaries had come to these areas, and decades later we are still seeing the fruition of what they planted because for seven years these Indians had to live in the most inhumane conditions, under garbage bags and with no running water or electricity. But they were patient and would not renounce their faith until the day came when God miraculously provided new land for them through the help of faithful brethren from Finland. More help came from Alaska when electricians and professionals in purifying water equipped the new little Indian village with purified running water and electricity. Most of the kids were suffering from parasites and mal-nutrition and Doctor Fernando, our friend, had already been out there with medication for them. When Albert and I arrived there, all the little children of the tribe wanted to play catch and other games with me. After a few hours of playing, when it started getting dark, I took the littlest boy with me by the hand and headed to where Albert was waiting in the little wooden, dirt floor church they had just built out of bamboo.

The rest of the thirty kids followed close behind. Albert sat the little boy on a chair next to him, and sure enough he had one leg a lot shorter than the other one. And it grew in the name of Jesus. One by one, the rest of the children began coming up for prayer. Pretty soon, moms with their babies started coming up for prayer and there was so much anointing that mostly everyone was healed of something. There is nothing that God can work with more than the heart of a child, and the place was full of children.

In another meeting in the city of Cali, Albert prayed for a teenage boy who had a mental disorder and could not talk. What Albert does when someone is unable to talk is that he gets them to sing. We all sang "Jesus Loves Me" to him, but the boy was not able to follow us. The next morning the boy's sister called up happy because her brother woke up singing!

I called the lawyer up and told him we had time to take him up on his request for us to go back to the city of Neiva to pray for the rest of his relatives and friends. Little did we know that this lawyer seemed to know half of the people in the city and they all needed prayer! We stayed for a night with the day completely full and our lawyer friend had to extend our flight ticket an extra day for more time. He took Albert and me from house to house, praying for the rich and the poor. We went from visiting million-dollar mansions to the most humble neighborhoods. People's faith grew so much that they started bringing Albert their pets.

One family brought him a cat, which had a broken leg and couldn't walk. When Albert prayed for the poor little kitty, the kitty immediately started to prance around the whole house! Five minutes before we had to leave for the airport we stopped at another house and a woman brought out a cage full of birds that needed prayer!

Albert prayed for the poor little birdies and we took off as soon as we could to the airport. More people were waiting for us when we got there. Albert quickly prayed for them. I especially remember the face of a sweet old woman that Albert prayed for. I didn't know what her sickness was, but I remember her face of pure gratitude as tears filled her eyes and she hugged us goodbye.

We went into the gate and found that our flight was delayed by forty minutes. I called the lawyer to tell him, and he talked to security personnel and they let us out to pray for more people while we waited for our flight. The lawyer must have called more of his friends because more people came to the airport! By the time Albert got done praying for all of them, the airport security guards wanted prayer too! So Albert started praying for all of them one by one.

Many had back problems. Airport maids started coming for prayer, and before we knew it, flight attendants of the airline were also asking for prayer.

We had time for a whole little revolution at the airport while we waited for our plane. We soon got back to our gate again, prayed for a few more flight attendants and security people inside, and then finally we were on our flight back to Bogotá. I had never before seen such a happy little airport.

A young guy who needed prayer picked us up from the airport and drove us to my house. Everything in his body was hurting and no matter how much Albert prayed for him, he didn't seem to improve. When he and his driver left our house, Albert and a friend from Alaska, Jon Dufendach, both got discernment from the Lord. The Lord showed them that the reason why this guy wasn't getting healed was because he was still holding on to something dark in his life.

A few hours later, a blind woman arrived at our house. Earlier she had called to ask my dad to speak at her church but instead my dad asked, "How is your health?" Immediately she took a cab as fast as she could to our home. She explained how several years earlier, she had had two tumors in her right eye and the doctors said that she would have to be operated on and that she would definitely lose her eye. She was in the hospital ready to go into surgery, but she didn't feel peace about it so she suddenly burst out of the operating bed and escaped the hospital and took a cab home! The Lord led her to a hospital that was run by a Christian doctor. He told her, "Look, I will be honest with you because I don't know if you will like this. The truth is that I place God and His wisdom first. He comes before all the books I've ever learned from and I am going to ask Him to give me wisdom as to how to operate on you and I will do as He shows me. Is that OK with you?" Well she was so happy. This was an answer to prayer. The Christian doctor operated on her and was able to take the two tumors out without having to eliminate her eye.

But days after her surgery she went out to her farm and met with country farmers who were suffering from a bad infection and she caught it as well. For six months, she had to endure an infection in her eye until it went completely dark, like a black screen. The other "good eye" was just old and so worn out that it didn't work very well either. When she told us the story about her eyes she said, "But my eyes are my secondary concern. What I really want is for the Lord to restore my first love for Him, because I feel I've lost it." Albert laid his hand on her eyes and began praying for her. When he stopped she said, "Pray a little more. I can see 90 degrees out of it, but I need to be able to see 130." So he prayed a little more. Then he stopped and she said, "OK. Now I can see but through what seem like spider webs." Albert said that what she was seeing were her own veins. He prayed that the blood pressure in the veins would return to normal in the name of Jesus and when he took his hand off her and she opened both of her eyes, she began to weep. I have never seen anyone so delighted in a miracle healing before!

Crying, she gasped, "My God, I can see! My God, thank you so much! I can see again! Marina, Alethia, I can see!" She called her husband up and said, "Honey, the Lord restored my vision. I can see!" Her husband, an orthopedic surgeon, started weeping on the other end of the telephone line. It was one of the most amazing moments I have ever witnessed! She was overjoyed. It was wonderful. Albert said to her, "Now you don't need to question your first love anymore, because you know that God loves you so much that He gave you back your eyes."

She invited us over to her church and Albert prayed for their whole congregation.

Then Russell took Albert to pray for the commanding general of the entire armed forces of Colombia. And the Lord healed him too.

The blind woman could now see again.

Letter to Senator Uribe

Dear Senator Alvaro Uribe Velez,

I am Albert W. Luepnitz, who gave you a message from the Lord in 2005.

Just as the Lord directed me in 2005 to prophesy to you that you were going to be reelected a second term as president and that the Lord would cause the constitution to be changed, so also, in January 2013, the Lord directed me to accompany Russell Martin Stendal to Cuba to address the FARC peace delegation.

The Lord had previously shown me that my grandfather, my father, and my brother were all controlled by a demon of anger (that actually killed my brother at age 42), and that they were victims, with no idea as to why. The Lord showed me that the FARC individuals were also victims driven by satanic forces they inherited from their parents.

When I addressed the FARC delegation in January 2013 (Ivan Marquez, Jesus Santrich, and Maritza), Russell and I saw deliverance of many demons from them. They observed the miracle healings that followed when I prayed for them, especially with Maritza, who was healed in the name of

Jesus of a very deformed right foot as a result of stepping on a mine that detonated. And she also had injuries in her left chest. Russell and I could see the change on the faces of these FARC individuals, as the darkness left, and was replaced by the light of Jesus Christ.

Since 1984, I have also prayed for and seen thousands of Colombian soldiers healed of combat injuries including blindness and deafness.

During the following two years, in several meetings with the FARC delegation, Russell and I addressed Pablo Catatumbo, Romana, Pastor Alape, Freddy, Yuri, and Noel. All were delivered of the satanic control on their lives and healed in the name of Jesus. They also accepted Jesus. They all genuinely voiced a desire to ask their victims to forgive them and they all voiced that they truly want peace in Colombia.

Senator Uribe, in 2005, the Lord demonstrated his authority and power to you and I am sure you realize this. On the 15th of November, 2014, the Lord directed me to return to Colombia to tell you the following: the Lord wants you to accept the fact that the individuals who killed your father were victims themselves, kidnapped by Satan himself to follow him in all their ways in directing the FARC organization. This is the reason for all the kidnappings and killings that followed. I want you to forgive them, says the Lord, to change direction, address the nation of Colombia and explain the above, as I have shown you. You are to lead this nation to forgiveness. If you do this, as I have directed, says the Lord, you will be known forever as the one that finally sealed peace in Colombia. I suggest you discuss this with President Santos.

On November 15th, I was advised by the Lord to convey the following message to you, Senator Uribe. You have to change direction and assist the president in the peace negotiations, particularly with the following stipulation:

The Lord has directed that the peace treaty must be negotiated God's way and not man's way, meaning complete and total forgiveness on both sides.

All hostiles must cease immediately.

You must confer with the president and try to reconcile your differences or else the peace treaty will not be signed and Marxist communists could put their candidate in for president and he or she might win if the two of you are divided. (An example of this is what happened in Bogotá in the past election for mayor.)

The peace treaty should in no way lead the country toward socialism or communism.

If a communist government takes over this country, there could be mass trials under the guise of human rights violations for the people who have opposed them.

Senator Uribe, I highly recommend that you abide by the above. The Lord has used you in the past in a mighty way and it was through His direct intervention that you became president a second term. What the Lord has in mind is for you to be a key player in finally establishing peace in Colombia along with the president.

I suggest a tentative peace agreement be done with the FARC to give you a sound basis to continue. Russell Stendal and I will be happy to assist you in any way we can in this endeavor.

In His service,

– *Albert W. Luepnitz*
The Lord's ambassador for peace in Colombia since 1984

A Prayer for Peace in Colombia

May 20, 2005

Dear generous and good Lord:

Our country Colombia wishes to speak to you with a grateful heart for having given us the most beautiful land, full of bright expectations but torn apart with trivial ambitions, quarreling, and disagreements. Please renew in us the spirit of reconciliation so that your voice persuades all men and women's hearts. Summon us to the virtues of charity, peace, and love so that we may deserve and receive your mercy. Make every one of us Colombians a messenger of truth, justice, and brotherly union in such a way that steadfast enemies may start speaking to each other again and old adversaries may stretch their hands in friendship. Where charity and tolerance overcome hate, where forgiveness defeats resentment and vengeance. Help us shatter the barriers of hostility and division and make us build together a fair and mutually binding nation.

Please make the civil authorities satisfy the fair hopes and wishes of the people and the ones that go through life without goals or objectives. Make the armed forces persevere in their demanding mission without losing heart in their task of building a durable peace and in seeking a renewed and promising horizon.

Keep the president of our country on his present path of progress, development, and justice for all Colombians. Help him to carry on the noble task of working for the common good. Keep him from evil events that may interfere with his good government and cast off all wicked and destructive spirits so we may forgive each other, heal past wounds and strive to improve the present unfair and continued suffering of our people.

Please send us the Holy Spirit so he changes our whole being, in constant search of the long awaited PEACE! PEACE! PEACE!

– Colonel (Retired) Armando Cifuentes Espinosa
President FIHNEC, Colombia

Albert's Colombia military escort

Albert praying for injured Colombian soldier

Maritza next to Albert showing off her new foot after she was healed
of serious injuries from stepping on a mine that exploded.

Pablo Catatumbo demonstrating to Albert
how he could not move his fingers

Pablo showing off his strong grip after he was healed

In December 2014, in Cuba, Albert prayed for the man standing between Russell and Albert. His name is Pastor Alape, one of
the FARC leaders. He received a miracle healing. With tears flowing, he asked permission to kiss Albert. He then kissed Albert on
the right cheek, saying, "I kiss you with love, like I would my father.
Thank you for praying for me. I too want peace in Colombia."

Miracles

A Miracle in a Difficult Pregnancy

In April 2013, our Cuban escort driver asked for prayer for his wife who was in the hospital experiencing a miscarriage at five months. When Albert prayed for her, she later said she actually felt the baby slide back into proper position and her womb close. At nine months the baby was five days past due. Clayton Sonmore, a visiting missionary friend of Russell's, prayed for her and the baby was delivered two hours later.

This family with Albert about a year later

Colombian Indian Healing Service
with Russell and Albert, 2013

Russell assisted me in praying for several thousand Colombian Indians. In this assembly, many with hernia problems, blindness, crossed eyes (wall eyes), scoliosis of the spine, one leg shorter than other, strokes, deafness, tumors, and cancer, knee- and foot problems were healed.

A FARC commander accompanied us through many miles of mountain ranges controlled by the FARC guerrillas, insuring safe passage to this meeting. This commander had stepped on a mine that exploded and was being treated for serious injuries to his foot. His foot was totally healed at this meeting. (This is the guerilla Alethia wrote about in her story.) Russell hired him to help us to arrive safely to the meeting before I would pray for him. Russell has another guerrilla friend now who will be a good witness to his troops about Jesus.

Seven undercover Indian police officers were in this group to protect Russell, myself, and the Christian Indian leaders from rebel Indians who were rumored to be attempting to infiltrate the meeting to kill us. I am not sure, but I think they were apprehended.

Indian Territory of Colombia

Final Testimonies

Report from Rev. Dr. Kebede F. Dibaba and Others, Fort St. John, BC, Canada

April 2013

Oh what a blessing to know you, Brother Albert! What a joy to welcome you into our home, our church, and our community! God is good and He is in charge. He knows all! Glory to His mighty name. Yes, the ministry was excellent. In town everyone talks about that. A lot of people received their healing. A woman who was carrying oxygen and couldn't breathe without it, was healed.

A woman named Barbara had a prior appointment scheduled with her doctor yesterday. When she learned he could not find anything wrong with her. She told him she went to a healing service. He clapped his hands, laughed, and said that was the best thing she could do.

A young boy who saw his mother, dad, and grandfather killed, now living with his grandmother, was seriously depressed and withdrawn. After several sessions with Albert, he was healed and is now a joyful boy.

Esther Haab reported that her mother had a good day referent the emphysema. Thanks for your prayers. At our Christian

Drug and Alcohol Rehab on our farm, one was healed from back pain. Another woman was healed of back pain that had been so severe she was going to quit her job. . Another 86-year-man was healed of a ruptured intestine.

Wanda Cummings. The meetings were excellent: many healings and some deliverances. I had never witnessed a short leg grow through prayer, but many, many did and the individual was healed. At the regular church service, with the permission of the parents, Albert lined the children up on the first pew and many, including their parents, were healed of scoliosis. One older girl walked in pushing a wheel-type chair in front of her. Her body was so twisted with scoliosis she could hardly walk. Albert ministered to her a couple of times and she got better, walking around on her own. Albert was very anointed but weary by the end of the evening.

On August 26, 2014, John Troyer of Fort St. John wrote that the previous Saturday afternoon, Jon Dufendach called him from Alaska, where Albert was visiting at his home. He told Jon that he had just hurt his knee very badly and was sitting in his chair with an ice pack on it. He was in a lot of pain and it was swollen badly. Jon asked Albert to pray for John over the phone, which he did. It was later, about 9:00 p.m. when John had to get out of his chair. He carefully started to move his leg he realized he was healed and no pain. By the next morning, all the swelling was also gone. Yes, God cares and thank you, Albert, for praying for me.

Cristina

Cristina lives in Bogotá and works at a Christian bookstore. She hated her grandmother because she left Cristina's mother and never loved her. Cristina's mother suffered a lot because of it. When Cristina was fourteen years old, her mother died, and at the funeral a sister of her grandmother asked her grandmother if she was going to take care of her granddaughter (Cristina) but the grandmother did not care. Cristina said to her grandmother, "If you did not care for your daughter, why would you take care of me?"

In 1992, Cristina began to have problems with her hands and after many exams, the doctors said she was OK but she could not open her hands unless she forced them open.

In 1993, she attended a meeting where Albert gave a teaching on how unforgiveness can cause physical and emotional problems. When Cristina forgave her grandmother, her deformed hands were suddenly healed.

On July 22, 2014, Cristina came to where Albert was staying in Bogotá and wanted prayer for severe lung infection, as it was hard for her to breathe. For three weeks, she went to different doctors and they gave her different medications but she did not feel any better. When Albert prayed for her, she was healed and said she had no more symptoms.

Pastors Cynthia and Mark Dillen, BC, Canada
September 2013

Albert touched many people's hearts and lives while here. His ministry has stirred up a deep hunger and thirst for more of God among His children but also fanned into flame…the dying embers in many hearts. I have had a number of calls from people asking if we have a mid-week service and when we're going to start the intercessory prayer group. People are definitely longing for a deep and wider manifestation of the Presence and Glory of God as well as a more intimate and passionate relationship with him!

It was an honor and a privilege to have you come and minister at our church and also spend time with us in our home. You are a very special brother in the Lord, who has poured himself liberally for the sake of the Kingdom. I know you bring the Father's heart much joy.

Stasia, my brother's girlfriend, who you prayed for, says her back still feels great … and the bump on her spine is gone.

I continue to have phone calls and e-mails from people thanking me for having you come and minister. Many lives were touched! Some received healings … others inner healing and release into forgiveness and the liberty that comes along with that. We had a number of people who came to salvation and those who rededicated their lives to the Lord after many years of "wandering in a far off land." It was so wonderful to look out in the congregation on Sunday and see new faces beaming back at me. In one row there were three people who came back to the Lord. One of the ladies in our congregation has been praying for her backslidden family for years. When she learned that Mark and I were fasting for an extended time preceding the special meetings with you … she also did for 10 days. Her daughter came out for the coffee house and brought her husband the next night. Then they came up for prayer with you and I believe he went down under the power of the Holy Spirit. They were both in church Sunday along with her son, who also rededicated his life to the Lord.

Janine Wolff, BC, Canada

April 18, 2013

I want to thank you and the Holy Spirit for the healing you placed on me Friday, April 12th, 2013. I was the woman who had a list too long to mention, then banged my head on the floor at the church as the church helpers did their best to lay me down.

I felt my body literally floating in the heat and light of God's hands. His energy was unbelievably calming to my soul. When I went to sleep that night I prayed for and thanked and thanked Jesus for his healing. I woke up the next day with "no" pain like

I felt before. It's great that you have found your purpose in life in all of God's plan.

Michael Poznekoff, Castlegar, BC, Canada

You prayed for a fellow on Skype. He had a disease where his eyes became crossed and then the left eye began to drift downwards and the right one was beginning to do the same. When you prayed, the eyes straightened out. You also prayed for his wife and at the beginning nothing appeared to happen, but now both her arm and leg are feeling much better.

You prayed for a young woman (Kelly) at the first house meeting and her back was healed. She was in a car accident in grade eight and was in pain. You prayed for her short leg to grow even with the other and her back to be straightened. Neck pain went away, posture straightened, and her friends say she looks taller.

A Russian Baptist evangelist came to your first meeting at Crescent Valley Hall and said that what you were doing was not right and that these things passed away with the apostles. On your final meeting at the Church of God he came forward for prayer for a brain tumor. When you prayed for him he fell to the floor and was still there when you left.

At the second house meeting you prayed for the hostess (Karen) because she had pain in her back, her hips, and she could not stand on her tip toes. She could not lift her heel off the ground when she stood. After prayer she felt better and then e-mailed saying, "Tell Albert that I just had my first pain-free walk."

Karen's daughter (Bailey) had pain in her back and a vertebrae on her neck stood out. When you prayed for her, the vertebrae went back in place and her back pain disappeared.

A Doukhobour woman (Polly) came forward on the final night due to back pain. When you prayed, the pain left immediately.

At Crescent Valley Hall, a fellow by the name of Kim had been in an accident and had pain in his back since then, over twenty years. After prayer, he was healed. Later the pain tried to return. Kim refused the pain and it stayed away.

John J. Closer, Major General (Retired) US Air Force

July 14, 2009

As commander of the 419th Tactical Fighter Wing at Hill Air Force Base in Ogden, Utah, I first became acquainted with Al (Albert W. Luepnitz). As a new Christian, I was skeptical of "holy roller" testimonies of miracles, but I went to a meeting where Al was speaking to check out his outlandish claims of healing back pain by "commanding" legs to align in the name of Jesus.

I specifically recall asking to put a straight ink pen line on the toe knuckles (which were definitely misaligned) of a man at the meeting whom I have known many years. I asked that he (the subject) not watch the effect of the prayer. Immediately, during the prayer, the two lines matched up. End of story for my doubting the reliability of the Bible and those that trust Him who wrote it. Al is a very different and focused guy. I would advise you take a chance (as I did) and test the claims made by him. What could you lose?

Rex, Mel, and the boys

November 18, 2013

We had a wonderful time in the Lord with you and fellow believers in Cottonwood, AZ in early October. We loved being in the presence of the Lord and hearing of the exploits of the Holy Spirit through your life.

Our family was physically blessed with healing power and physical issues changed and continue to remain so.

My wife, Melanie, had a severe break in her right ankle

several years ago. Two major reconstructive operations left her with diminished function and pain in her leg. She had seven breaks and required eleven screws and plates to stabilize the leg. It was atrophied and muscle mass diminished. We drew a line across both feet before you prayed. Her leg grew out and changed position so that the lines that were once touching were now separated by an inch. The atrophy in the right leg was corrected and the dimension of the soft tissue of that leg also changed as new depth of flesh appeared around the old incisions.

Our 13-year-old, Christian, had a spine issue that caused him to lean to the right out of habit. You prayed and the Lord lengthened his right leg, restoring stability. You prayed for his spine and a change occurred to the curvature of his lower spine.

You prayed for Caleb's legs and they equalized.

Sammy. He was fine. He felt so important as you blessed him and anointed him for service.

Rex. You prayed for my ears that needed a creative miracle to restore nerves lost during sickness as a child. I received relief and continue to receive steady improvement. I believe this is an example of therapy healing that Jesus performed many times. He would say go to the high priest and show yourself. As they went in obedience, they received their healing. So do I.

Albert, you are a precious gift to the Body of Christ. We count it a blessing and favor from the Lord to know you and have you in our life. We love to hear from you and believe for every rich manifestation of the Covenant to be fulfilled in your life.

Lauri Mason, Agape Ministries, Escanaba, Michigan.

On June 13, 2010, my eleven-year-old son Kevin was healed of ADHD, the beginning of scoliosis and also bipolar disorder. He felt some bones pop back in place in his neck and his face lit up. He also saw God lengthen his right leg about one inch.

Since that day Kevin has been off all medications and was given a clean bill of health from his doctor. He tells everyone what Jesus has done for him. He is a very different kid. We are praising God for sending Brother Albert to our church.

Paul F. Corbett, Major (Retired) US Air Force
July 16, 2009

July 20th, 1984, is when I first met Albert W. Luepnitz. It was at a Full Gospel Businessmen's Fellowship International luncheon. During the meeting, he gave his testimony saying he was destined to be in a wheelchair for life. But God healed him.

At the meeting, he prayed for me. He did not know that I had swollen arteries on both sides of my neck; eventually this caused me pain and migraine headaches every eight hours. When he prayed for me, he put both hands on my neck arteries. In approximately two minutes, all swelling disappeared and I have had no pain since, which was twenty-five years ago. I am alive today because of the power of God's Holy Spirit, which healed me through the hands and faith of Albert W. Luepnitz.

As president of our chapters, we have invited Albert to speak over the past twenty-five years. We have seen miracles upon miracles through his ministry. This man, I believe, is one of the most anointed men of God in healing.

Jim Manning, Coach and
Teacher, Longview, Texas

Our daughter, Jaclyn, was diagnosed with leukemia in her senior year of high school in 2011. My wife and I taught in the same school district that our daughter attended. We drove the four hours to MD Anderson Hospital, Houston, Texas, about thirty times during her senior year for chemo treatment and stayed for thirty days the first time she went.

I was introduced to Albert at a church in Longview, Texas,

several months before Jaclyn was diagnosed. I sensed one day, since Albert lived right outside of our hometown, that I would call Albert and set up a time for him to pray for our daughter on our way to treatments in Houston.

My daughter and I stopped at his home. As Albert ministered to Jaclyn, I sensed a very strong anointing while he was praying. I truly believe that day Jaclyn was totally healed of leukemia. It was very soon after that, that Jaclyn's vitals were normal.

I was so full of joy and the Holy Spirit that on the way to Houston I was stopped twice for speeding; the second time I received a ticket.

At MD Anderson Hospital they verified Jaclyn was totally healed of leukemia. Now, three years later at age twenty-two, Jaclyn is still 100 percent healed and serving God at Life Bridge Christian Center in the college department.

I also believe I received an impartation of healing that same day when Albert prayed for Jaclyn.

Guatemala

In October 2014, I received a message from a friend in Guatemala asking me to pray for the four-year-old daughter of Jorge and Cinthia Garcia.

I received an e-mail from Jorge, who explained their daughter Luciana was diagnosed with cancer, specifically synovial sarcoma in her right foot. The doctors recommended surgery to amputate the foot.

We arranged a date and time for me to pray for Luciana by telephone. I prayed for her, commanded in the name of Jesus for the cancer to die. On October 29, 2014, I received an e-mail from Jorge confirming that Luciana was healed of the foot cancer.

Mary Erickson, Gladstone, Michigan

It was in September of 2014, when we were all in the van riding to a little town in Upper Michigan called Gaastra. That is where I first met Albert.

I was new to the area, but my brother lives here, and I had recently moved in with him. I had heard a lot about "Uncle Albert." He was our pastor's uncle and he had the gift of "working of miracles." Many people in the church had received healings from him and I knew I had to meet him. The church was praying for Albert because he had been sick and in the hospital. My prayer was, "Lord, please don't take him yet. I have to meet him. Please make a way for him to be healed and make a trip up here." The Lord answered that prayer.

I found Albert to be a man in his 80s, medium stature, thin, and wearing glasses. He was very open to his past, easy to talk to. He wasn't anything special to look upon but he was very special as a vessel of God. He told me of his ministry in Colombia for approximately thirty years, working miracles with the striving leadership there. We talked, we connected, and I waited to see what God would do when we arrived at the Mission Bible Training Camp in Gaastra, Michigan.

The mission, to my understanding, is a place where people end up as almost a last resort to receive healing from addictions, hurts, and wounds from living a hard life in this world. There were mostly young people there, in their twenties and up. As I looked at their faces, I could see the hardness and skepticism, yet at the same time a slight glimmer of hope was hidden behind their eyes, and Albert was there to make it grow and grow it did. He spoke of his testimony, of the healings that had taken place in the jungles of Colombia, and how the anointing of the Holy Spirit brought about great changes there. He wanted to pray for some of the gals in the front row but they were somewhat timid, until one stood up. She was a heroin addict and this was her second time at the mission. This time she was serious and Albert prayed for her. The Holy Spirit was beginning *His* work. A young man, tall and thin, his hair in dreadlocks, wanted Albert to pray for his back. Albert asked him, "What do you do?" And the young man answered, "I am a thug." Albert sat him in the chair, noticing that one leg was longer than the other. He commanded the short leg to grow and it did. The man stood up and Albert prayed for the vertebrae in his back and the man was healed. The young man began twisting and touching his toes, and jumping; he was ecstatic. Albert asked him what was wrong with his back. He said he had been shot with a 40-caliber bullet. That was one of the many healings that night. After that man was healed, many wanted prayer and to be touched by the Lord, and they were.

Sunday morning at church Albert began ministering again, and this time it was my turn. I wanted my back to be healed and I wanted this anointing that he had. He sat me down; my legs were not even; and one leg grew just as it was commanded to do in the name of Jesus. I stood up and I can hardly explain the sweet anointing. It was pure, undefiled love, and it penetrated my spirit where I was born again several years ago. I never felt such a strong presence of love and I went down on the floor where the Lord began healing me from all the hurts and wounds that had recently taken place in my life.

I had a hard time saying goodbye to this gentleman who made a strong impact on my life. Through the gift of the Holy Spirit I knew there was a bond of unity in the Spirit and that bond was Jesus working through him. It's hard to explain.

I gave Albert a hug and stared into his eyes for a moment, looking for that last glimpse of Jesus. He looked right through me and said, "You're precious." I know it was from the Lord.

Thank you, Albert. May God bless you and keep you.

Carl Lambeck, Gaastra, Michigan

I remember the first time we had Albert come to the Mission Bible Training Camp with us, in Gaastra, Michigan, where we saw many healings. One that I remember was a young girl named Carrie. She was addicted to drugs and smoking cigarettes, I think. She received an instant healing and was delivered completely from her addictions.

Another one was a man, who I believe was injured in a motorcycle accident and had part of the bone in his lower leg removed, resulting in one leg being shorter. He too asked for prayer and was healed at once as both legs became the same length.

Another healing that blessed us was a young woman from Philadelphia, who had a severe back pain. Albert sat her down and had as many as could come around her to witness God's love and His power become not only heard, but also seen, at work. The girl had a leg that was four to six inches shorter than the other. When Albert commanded it to grow to the same length as the other in Jesus' name, it did so immediately. All were amazed at God's grace. I remember this woman, whose name was Jessica, got up and said, "I feel different. I feel different. I feel wonderful."

I think the greatest blessing was the healing of faith of these young Christian people. They had read about miracles and heard about miracles, which encouraged their hope in God's word, but seeing the love and power of the Holy Spirit working in them and those around them brought life to their faith. We saw faith come alive in new Christians and renewed faith in old ones so they become more than conquers in Christ, even more than the physical healings.

Frank Koch

About four or five years ago a friend told me Albert was going to be in Schuyler, Nebraska, at his church. Albert would be praying for people with health needs. Having a religious background of questioning – and scoffing – at such things, yet knowing reputable people experienced physical healing, I decided to go to observe. After giving his testimony, Albert asked if any wanted to be ministered to. I decided to let him pray for my macular degeneration, which I have had for a number of years in my left eye. Also I had several weak disks in my lower vertebra and my back out of place from lifting something too heavy and had constant pain from a nerve as a result. When Albert prayed for me – in Jesus' name – the pain immediately ceased and over these years has never returned. All Glory to God

Mary Zeiset

November 26, 2014

A few weeks before our wedding, my husband and I were informed that I had hypothyroidism and a goiter with a nodule on it. I started taking meds but I still struggled with infertility for three years.

After the birth of our second child, my levels started fluctuating and I had to quit my medication. We started searching for other options besides drugs, all the while praying for healing. During this time, Albert came through the area. After putting his hand on my throat and commanding in the name of Jesus that my thyroid function normally, I felt my thyroid shrink. Three months later, I had another blood test and the results came back normal!

Pam Sonmore

On September 20, 2013, Alethia sent me an e-mail asking me if I could pray for a friend of hers, Pam Sonmore, in Portland, Oregon. She said Pam has a tumor in her thyroid and facing surgery. Pam also has Hashimoto Disease, which is an autoimmune disease. I just happened to be traveling in Portland with my daughter. We went by and saw Pam.

When I prayed for Pam, I placed my fingers on her obviously swollen thyroid. I felt the tumor and swelling leave. Pam told Alethia that I prayed for her and appeared to be healed.

I later received a telephone call from her father, Clayt Sonmore, and he said that it was verified that Pam was totally healed.

Mike Maxwell

On October 15th, 2012, I (Albert) was returning home from a church meeting where I had a healing service.

I had a strong discernment from the Lord that Mike, my pastor, had a serious blood vessel blockage and that I should pray for him. I telephoned Mike and prayed for him.

The following morning I received an e-mail from him. He was at the hospital. Mike said he knew he had a blockage and that the Lord healed him. Right after this he said he heard the message, "To whom much is given, much is expected!" Mike gave all glory to God.

Mike said, "Thank you for your healing prayer and may God continue to bless you."

As usual, I cried a little, thanking the Lord…

Steve Krahn

I attended Lutheran school K-8 and played college hockey for Minnesota State. I engaged in extreme drug use from 16-36 years of age and overdosed eight times. Shot by guns on three different occasions, I should be dead. The last caused paralysis from waist down, and Mom pushed me in a wheelchair to church twenty-eight days later. I wasn't thrilled. I was depressed and high on pills and heroin. After church people prayed for me. Supposedly I was never to walk again. (Doctor's opinion.) Two days later, I was walking with a cane. Praise God.

The night Albert prayed for me at MBTC. I had been in Gaastra one week. I was walking without a cane at the time. There was a lot of pain and discomfort in my spine from the bullet wound and it still hurt to walk. After Albert prayed over me in the name of Jesus and I could move normally again. I could squat, sit, and walk without a limp. I have not had any pain or limp since and I thank the Lord every day for my legs and so much more.

(Note: From Pastor Art Kievit, Agape Ministries Church, Escanaba, Michigan. I minister at this mission on a regularly monthly schedule. Several months later Steve is doing good with constant improvement spiritually and does not look or act like he was ever hurt.)

Note

These numerous testimonies merely give you a picture of what our wonderful Jesus can do – no limits, ask believing, staying in tune to the Spirit to discern root problems. Albert was faithful to "live Jesus" and move in his giftings.

This could only have been realized since Albert maintained a pure heart and clean hands with God. This leaves us with the same challenge – what can and will He do through us? Jesus is no respecter of persons. If we are "clean" He will pour out grace and giftings and we shall "make a difference." We need to keep faith over feelings, trust over fear, and truth over opinion. A wise old saint said it well:

Give a man a word from God and he's inspired for a day,
Teach a man to hear from God and he's inspired for a lifetime.

Albert hears from God and so must we, in order be a partaker instead of a spectator. Go and do likewise...

Letter from Jesus Santrich

I n March 2015, Russell told me that the FARC delegation at the peace conference in Cuba wanted to meet me in Cuba. Ivan, the head of the FARC peace negation team explained to me that he and a few other FARC delegates wanted to see me, not just for prayer, but to personally thank me for all the Lord did for them through my ministry.

Ivan advised that the first word from the Lord that I gave him on October 12, 2014 had become a reality in his life, giving him divine revelation that is affecting the direction of the peace talks. Ivan also advised that in April 2013, when I told him that the Lord said the peace treaty had to be the Lord's way, not man's way, or it would fail, saved the peace negotiations – the FARC were ready to quit and go home.

On 30 March 2015, Jesus Santrich, one of the main leaders of the FARC delegation who received miracle healings for epilepsy and other problems, wrote the following letter:

The Love of God as the Way to Peace
A message of gratitude for our missionary friends of love and peace. (Translation)

Thanks to Grandfather Albert for having shown us that God has his heart full of love for all humanity. He does not love some more or less, God simply and marvelously loves us all equally. But we need to respond so that his Divine Grace can completely penetrate our existence; we must open our conscience from each spark of reason we receive that we might live, in the midst of disappointments and happiness, in the midst of success and failure, in the midst of optimism and frustration, and even more in the midst of need than in the midst of abundance; because these are the challenges and trials that we must sort through with solidarity and equanimity to show forth the true dimension of our hearts.

Thanks to Grandfather Albert for teaching us by opening our consciences and readying our feelings to assume a life of sacrifice, thinking more of our neighbors than ourselves, reviving the communion of all of us and assuming everyone as our brothers, that this will allow us to deserve the fullness of the love of God, this will make our goals possible and position us to be deserving of the fulfillment of these goals.

Thanks to Grandfather Albert for being a missionary of love and of faith in a future filled with goodness and in which the highness of God is imperative. Thanks to Albert, and also Martin (Russell Stendal), to his children, to all his family and to their friend (Luis) Humberto, for showing us their profound and interested human affection and that there is no darkness along our path if the light of God is on fire in our souls.

Signed: *Jesus Santrich*

For me, this perhaps is not the final conclusion of my more than thirty years in Colombia seeking peace that has been going on since 1964, but it at least is the best chance so far. In October 2013, because of extreme fatigue, I was going to quit going to Cuba and Colombia. However, a visiting pastor in a church I was visiting, said the Lord told him to tell me I could not quit as HE still needed me in Cuba and Colombia. This pastor knew nothing previously about me, so it had to have been inspired by the Lord. I thank the Lord because what followed might never have happened.

WHAT AN ADVENTURE WITH JESUS IT HAS BEEN

P.S. March 2017, just returned from Bogota where I met with my friend, Jesus Santrich. He came for dinner at Russell's and we spent the evening together. Afterwards we went into the next room and he related something profound: *"Albert, I love you. I still cannot see, but I have a new set of eyes inside and now I see totally different."*

Albert with Jesus Santich

Reflections and Continuing Adventure, April 2017

*F*or God sent not his Son into the world to condemn the world, but that the world through Him might be saved, (John 3:17). Hear this, for it is God's desire to pour out His love and power to all who will listen.

In March 2015, as previously mentioned, Ivan, FARC leader and head of their peace delegates wanted to see Russell and me. He told me something very interesting, "We did not accept Jesus only because of the miracle healings when you prayed, not from the Word you and Russell spoke but because of the way you presented yourself."

This made me think; so during subsequent prayer, the Lord showed me what Ivan was talking about. The following addition to what was previously said will detail an area in my life that was never mentioned before.

After leaving home in 1943 under some very dire circumstances, I was drafted into the US army. After basic training, I had various assignments, and then was stationed at a military base in Wisconsin in the latter part of 1945. I had been promoted in rank and was assigned to various duties. I met another soldier a lot older than me. One weekend he invited me to accompany him to Milwaukee. He told me he was a member of the mafia, an organization specializing in many criminal activities, including murder. For about eight months, I attended many meetings and met the top local leaders and made a token agreement of accepting membership, including what I would do when discharged. Interestingly, I met an Army officer at my base that was also a mafia figure.

This officer had me transferred to the Military Police so that I could be in a position to assist in allowing stolen military clothing to be transported through gate security to leave the base. I was receptive to this mafia organization since I still had an issue of anger about getting expelled from school and from my home circumstances, and had ideas of serious retaliation against my dad and those who lied about me or did not volunteer the truth. This organization would offer financial security and make possible the ideas of revenge. My plan was that as soon as I was discharged from the Army, I would, in the middle of the night, set fire to every home in Moran of those who lied about me or knew the truth but did not speak up when I was wrongly expelled from school.

However, before any of the above could manifest, a senior master sergeant that I worked with said he needed to talk to me. He did not know about the above plans but he obviously recognized I had serious problems. This sergeant conversed with me for a few minutes before saying, "Luepnitz, if you would straighten up your act, you could amount to something." This was the first good advice I ever recalled anyone ever saying to me – and it had a deep affect.

Previously it was explained in this book how I re-enlisted in the US Army and what occurred afterwards, including how I walked out of the world of darkness. What the devil meant for evil, God has used for good.

Therefore, returning to March of 2015 when Ivan said, "It

was not the healings or the spoken Word why we accepted Jesus; it was the way you presented yourself!" This really got my attention. What was I presenting?

I asked Ivan what he meant. His reply, "You accepted us, you didn't look down at us as being inferior. You projected understanding, acceptance and love.

I asked, "How did you understand that, I never put it in spoken words?"

Ivan replied, "*It is something we can feel when around you.*"

Then I remembered what my friend Russell would say when he introduced me at speaking engagements, "Albert has a very humble spirit..." The dealings and love of God had now brought me to that place of no condemnation. Its effect, by the Spirit, had allowed Ivan and others to perceive, to feel, to identify.

I understood what was happening. It was an application of a spiritual transfer from me without the need of speaking. It was also the reason why many people in the years of my ministry in Colombia, and now including Ivan and a number of other FARC leaders, had healings manifested and demons expelled in my presence without verbally commanding them.

One other very significant happening occurred during this time together in Cuba. Initially I had a heart and mind struggle. How can I love those hardened guerillas? It's one thing to speak healing in Jesus' name; but it is quite another to face the challenge of loving the unlovely. However, Russell was able to do it – there were seemingly no barriers to his love! What was my roadblock, the obstacle to spiritual breakthrough?

Healings opened the door but not enough to change them. A heart-opening epiphany came gradually. At some point in time, however, I saw it and I felt it. Actually happened when I embraced Russell's "heavenly view" which was revolutionary: *He saw these guerillas not as they were, but rather as they could be!* Yes, Russell saw them by faith as they could be through grace – an awesome difference, allowing him to love them for what they could be. So these atheist Communist guerillas first opened their minds to the reality of God, then opened their hearts to the love of Jesus. They became our brethren, as it so beautifully states in 1 John 3:16, *"Hereby perceive we the love of God, because he laid down his life for us; and we ought to lay down our lives for the brethren."* All glory to God!

Our friend David Witt, also a missionary statesman and founder of Spirit of Martyrdom, has come alongside Russell's ministry in recent years and given wonderful support in many ways. His thoughts follow and give a perspective and overview of the history and happenings that have unfolded, particularly with regard to my joining Russell in the Peace Process and related ministry outreaches.

David Witt, Spirit of Martyrdom

I want to share some history about Albert Luepnitz' participation in Latin America and serving alongside Russell Stendal. The Lord partnered Albert and Russell in these latter days for spiritual harvest just like Barnabas and Paul. I have witnessed the gospel being revealed to many (Colombian) government officials, soldiers and people not only by His word but with His working through Albert and Russell. (1 Thessalonians 1:5)

In early 1980s the doctors told Albert that he would soon be in a wheelchair from an incurable degenerative back disease. The Lord miraculously healed Albert when he was prayed for by a Christian worker. In 1981, the Lord called Albert to minister in Latin America. It was not until May of 2009 that Russell and Albert met in person. Russell translating for Albert at a luncheon held for Colombian officers. Sometime after this first meeting Albert prayed for Alethia, Russell's daughter, since she was having back pain from scoliosis. Alethia was immediately healed and many other family members have been healed since.

In 2010, Russell and Alethia began interpreting for Albert during his ministry visits to Colombia. They were able to witness hundreds of Colombians being healed of spiritual and physical needs in the name of Jesus. Russell expressed that Albert was very humble by giving all glory to God, never asking for money and would pay his own way on the ministry trips. Albert understands that God is sovereign and he accepts that God sometimes heals and sometime He does not. God used Albert as a conduit of grace and truth in Jesus Christ. His main message proclaimed God is the one who touches people and heals because of His great love for all mankind and that lost souls would be reconciled with their heavenly Father.

During 2012, the movie La Montana, was released by Lisa Stendal-Hernandez and Alethia Stendal. It highlights Russell's relationship with a FARC guerilla commander, Noel. The movie portrays how Noel was once a soldier who guarded Russell during his five-month captivity and now is a trusted friend by the power of forgiving your enemies. The Colombian Peace Accord negotiations held in Havana, Cuba between the Colombia Government and the FARC guerrilla leadership began in 2013 and Noel was a part of the guerrilla delegation in Cuba. From Noel's recommendation, Russell received an invitation to meet with the guerrilla leadership and brought a copy of the film La Montana. When the leaders viewed the film, it built credibility for Russell and Albert and showed that the power of God can make peace where there is no human hope for peace.

In preparation for this first visit, Russell prayed about how to handle this historic invitation to finally meet with the top guerrilla leadership. This invitation was a culmination of 35 years of ministry in Colombia; Russell distributed millions of Christian books in the guerilla-controlled area including night flights dropping materials and radios via parachutes and had installed multiple radio stations and broadcasts. The cost to Russell was three attempts by the guerrillas to assassinate him and five times taken hostage and temporarily held. The guerrilla leaders knew Russell's story and had heard gospel teachings. Now they needed a demonstration of the power of Christ. As Russell prayed about this first meeting with the guerrillas in January 2013 he was led to invite Albert. Albert joined Russell and they had a major breakthrough during the first encounter. Five of the guerrilla leaders were dramatically healed of physical needs which led them to open their minds and hearts to the teaching of the Word of God by Russell. They kept the meetings and conversations of faith with the guerrillas discreet for the first three years.

In April 2013, the Lord directed Albert to urgently return to Cuba with Russell and he told the delegate, "This says the Lord, peace has to be God's way, not man's way or it will fail." Russell was told the FARC delegates were beginning to be discouraged and were going home. However, when they heard the message from Albert, they decided this was from the Lord, which led them to stay the course of the peace process. After Albert returned home to Texas, he was feeling drained physically, spiritually and mentally. He had ministered over thirty years in Colombia and was considering his travel and ministry season had come to a close. A pastor who met Albert for the first time and did not know Albert's ministry to Latin America, spoke prophetically encouraging him to "continue God's work in Cuba and Colombia."

Albert continued to travel to Cuba with Russell many times and several FARC generals received healing and accepted Jesus as their savior.

David Witt
www.spiritofmartyrdom.com

Albert and Russell in Colombia

Two missionary statesmen who hear from God and whose actions have impacted a nation...

Albert went to Cuba under the auspices of *Spirit of Martyrdom* and was given the code name of Grandpa...

Testimonies of Divine Encounters

Jaime Ruiz, Colombia

It´s been almost 12 years that I was called to be the translator of Albert Luepnitz in one of the annual conferences held by the Full Gospel Businessmen Fellowship. At that time I was not familiar with anything God-related or with miracles and healings. I started to translate at Albert´s meetings more as an adventure than really working consciously for God. The years passed, I started studying the Word and gave my life to Jesus, and saw hundreds of miracle healings while I was with Albert.

As a Catholic, I once invited Albert to go to a mass held by a priest friend, Father Jaime, a charismatic religious man who developed a relationship with us. I was in charge with the priests of a prayer group which was held every Thursday at the parish auditorium. Albert came often and I witnessed many times the power of God through healings and deliverances. We saw how tumors and cysts just disappeared in people. But I believe that one type of miracle that struck Father Jaime was to see minors grow!

These children grew up to three inches. It was incredible. We told the children to lie against a wall, and we put a mark on the wall. We asked them how much they wanted to grow. Then

Albert ordered them to grow the centimeters that the children had said grow in the name of Jesus. We watched as they grew before our eyes. But that was not all – even the clothes grew with them. Children who grew showed their astonishment and gratitude to almighty God…All to His glory

Colombian General Rodrigues, Retired

General Rodrigues saw me at Russell's home asking for prayer for terminal cancer. Shortly thereafter, I had him share his testimony that his doctors confirmed the healing at a church in Bogota where I was invited to minister. At this meeting there were about twelve cancer patients in the attendees wanting prayer. Most of them could feel the tumors and when I addressed their problem, the tumors left and they could no longer feel them.

Pastor Clarence, Ft Smith, Arkansas

November 30th, 2015: Brother Albert, many wonderful things were manifested in our service as a result of the gifts God blessed you with and has entrusted to you. My mom was scheduled for double knee replacement on December 14th. Since your prayer, she has canceled the surgery. My son, Elijah, has had constant feet pain dealing with his deformities, many surgeries have not corrected any of his problems, but only made the issues worse. Since the prayers, he has had no pain. This is enough to make me shout! My son of 18 years is finally free of constant pain.

Sister Trudy was involved in an 18-wheeler accident resulting in a steel plate in her back and neck area. This limited her mobility severely. Since the prayer, she is able to move her neck from side to side and up and down without any limitations! Mike Reeves, my associate pastor, had crippling knee pain. Since the prayer no pain at all!

Alethia, Russell's daughter

On 18 April 2016, I was Albert's interpreter at my dad's home in Bogota. Albert was ready to return home. The lady that previously had been blind and healed when Albert prayed for her as previously mentioned, brought her husband , a surgeon to have Albert pray for him. This doctor had a brain tumor and it was causing him to lose his mind. Albert rebuked the tumor, commanded it to die in the name of Jesus, the doctor immediately had it checked.

Later I reported the results to Albert: They cannot fine the tumor, it is gone. Also, his mind is clear.

Oskar and Margo Greiner, Vancouver, BC, Canada

Having flown from Dallas, Texas on April 2, 2013 Albert was barely through the door of Oskar and Margo Greiner's Burnaby home when two of Margo's rehabilitation clients arrived for healing prayer. One woman in her early forties had sustained serious head and orthopedic injuries one year earlier. She was unable to work as a teacher. While she was not instantly healed, she later reported that over the course of six months, she improved significantly. She reported that her medical team and the school district cited this recovery as a miracle. To God be the glory!

At Interdenominational Pastor's prayer fellowship, Vancouver, there were about twenty present. Seven claimed they received a miracle healing of various foot conditions and one of neuropathy. This was noteworthy, as all were missionaries and pastors.

Albert prayed for about thirty people at our house meetings. Each one who received prayer reported a touch from Jesus. One pastor with a degenerated hip joint reported pain improvement. Jesus healed depression. Legs were lengthened and backs were healed. Aubrey, a man in his forties had feet that were a different size, and he always had to buy a different shoe size for each foot. Through Jesus' healing power, both feet are now identical in size.

Petronel, a woman in her thirties, had suffered back pain for years. She could garden for only one hour and the next day she would have back pain. Through Albert's prayer and Jesus' healing power, she felt her leg growing. For two weeks thereafter she had back pain, as though her back was adjusting to her pelvis being aligned. After two weeks, there was no more pain and no more limitations.

Amie, who had a long history of depression and mental instability, received prayer. In follow up Amie wrote that she was honored to be at the gathering and it really made a huge difference in her life, both physically and mentally. Now for the first time in five years, she was able to enjoy the simpler things of life that she had forgotten, or was too depressed to see… like flowers, butterflies and hummingbirds. She went to the garden early and sang. Jesus' healing touch permeated her spirit and body. We give Jesus all the glory for His love and healing power in each person's life!

Jason Roads, Jacksonville

It was the first time I had heard of something like this and didn't pay much attention, especially since it was mostly happening in Colombia. I was grateful for knowing what God was doing but didn't think it would ever involve me. In May of 2016, I heard Albert was coming back. I thought *"Okay, I will go see what this guy is all about."* He was speaking to a group of 60-70 teens that were interested in foreign missionary work. What I saw in that church auditorium shook my faith in a hugely positive way.

In all honesty, as Albert began to heal people of back pain, shoulder problems, and a myriad of other physical ailments, I thought for a few fleeting moments that maybe, just maybe, these kids were acting or perhaps invited to act this way to mislead others. However, I quickly snapped back to reality and realized that this was pure and harmless and that God was truly working in the room.

I saw healing after healing and finally decided to leave after I saw a young girl receive an incredible healing right in front of my eyes. Her hips severely pointed inwards so much so that when she walked her thighs and knees were completely together and she hobbled badly. After receiving prayer, she stood up. Albert commanded her to walk and after 2-3 short steps, her thighs opened in front of my eyes. She was speechless and the room was too. I knew it was a miracle because she was 10 years old and I saw her mother nearly fall to the ground in tears of joy. You cannot fake this and who would anyway.

When I left that room, I felt like I walked into thinner air and I nearly started crying. I was hooked on the power of healing that the Holy Spirit gives. Later that day I saw many more people healed through Albert, including my wife who had scoliosis and my daughter who had a short leg by a few inches.

Albert returned in early September. I decided to follow this man around town throughout the week and again saw many, many healings of backs, shoulders, knees, ankles, many curses were broken, and emotional strain and depression was lifted. For the first time I had Albert pray over me multiples times. I was healed instantly on three occasions and another time achieved full healing within 1 hour of the prayer.

Mike Elin, Jacksonville, Florida

As it turned out, there were small groups who filed in and out all that morning. There were generally somewhere between one to two dozen individuals present at a time. As before, many of those present were encouraged to get close enough to be able to watch as people with leg, spine, back and shoulder issues were being healed. Albert often would take a little time for a teaching moment. Other times he would never hesitate to suggest practical measures regarding forgiveness, diet or lifestyle choices or supplementing one's diet where there may be problems due to deficiencies. However, there was one situation that arose that morning that Albert had never encountered before.

A family of four came in around mid- morning. The father was healed of shoulder and back issues, and the daughter who was about eight years old had just seen her short leg lengthened. After a little pause, she rolled her eyes and exclaimed out loud to the chuckles of some present, "That was weird!" She then stood while Albert began to minister to her mom. Right in the middle of this the little girl suddenly turned around toward her father with an expression of terror on her face and cried out "It went dark! It went dark!" She had just gone stone blind! Her dad scooped her up in his arms and was now visibly shaken. The concern among those in attendance was becoming palpable. Albert quickly attended to the situation with the little girl. This was an overt demonic assault designed to disrupt the meeting and instill fear in those who were in attendance. Albert rebuked the spirit in the name of Jesus and the little girl's eyesight briefly returned, but she complained of a terrible ringing in her ears. Albert suggested that they take her just outside the chapel into the fresh air. But as their family was about to go out the chapel's back double doors the little girl cried out and went totally blind again - interrupting ministry a second time. Now we joined the family outside as the rest of those present remained inside and quietly discussed what was happening or prayed. By this time the entire family was very scared. The older teenage brother was so upset that he was visibly trembling as he stood next to me. Dad again held the little girl who was facing him as Mom anxiously peered over his shoulder into her daughter's face. Albert, in the name of Jesus, then bound the spirit, loosed the little girl from its power and commanded it to leave. The girl's eyesight immediately returned and she relaxed in her father's arms. From their vantage point the parents later described to me that while their daughter had been blind, her skin was ashen – devoid of any color. Her eyes were completely dilated. When the demonic presence left, her color suddenly returned and her eyes returned to normal. The family remained for a little while then left to go home, and Albert went back into the chapel for a little teaching moment. Within an hour the family returned, and as they led their daughter by the hand up the walkway they were absolutely beaming with smiles that went ear to ear. They turned into the chapel to share additional good news with everyone who was present.

Apparently, their daughter had been demonstrating "behavior problems" for some time. After they returned home, their little girl was the calmest and sweetest individual she had ever been. Apparently, she had undergone a complete change of personality. Now they returned to share the wonderful news with everyone; we were all very grateful that they had done so. The mother of one SSUMC staff member present that morning later remarked that if she had entertained even the slightest doubt as to the validity of either Albert's ministry or the reality of the demonic realm, it instantly vanished as she personally witnessed the sobering events of that morning.

Thankfully, Albert moved calmly and firmly to handle the crisis or it would have been a disaster. Later he related several personal thoughts about this incident. First, although he had witnessed a large variety of demonic manifestations over many years, this was the first time that a demon had ever manifested itself as an attack of blindness on a child. Second, he was relieved that although the group in the chapel had shown great concern about the situation, no one had "gone through the brick wall" in attempting to make an exit for themselves. Third, he made the rather frightening observation, that if the situation had not been handled properly by someone who knew how to move with spiritual authority, then that little girl possibly may have remained permanently blind.

Chris Cosper, September, 2016

Last year I had the pleasure of having Albert attend a men's Bible study I am part of through my church in Jacksonville, Florida. There were about 8 to 10 men in my small group listening to the story of how he received his gift and stories of healing. I was hoping there might be opportunity to ask questions as I was curious if he could tell when someone was in need, or if they had to approach him. That question was answered when he stopped, looked directly at me, and asked what sort of issue I was having with my back.

At 53 years, I'm a regular jogger with a physically demanding job that requires lots of lifting. For about a year, I suffered from a problem with my shoulder and upper back that prevented me from lifting things over my head with my right arm. I was unable to throw a football or baseball without pain.

Albert asked me to come around the table, sit down in a chair and extend my legs straight out. My right ankle was clearly one and a half inches above the left. With the other men in my group circled around, Albert supported my feet and stated clearly "in the name of Jesus, align these legs." As I sat perfectly still, we all watched my ankles line up in only a few seconds.

He said leg length is often the basis for back issues and was possibly the cause of my problem. Next, he asked me to stand and show him where my shoulder issue was. He then gave me a sort of bear hug, and again prayed for healing in the name of Jesus. I actually felt my spine move. If anyone had known to watch, I believe they would have seen my shirt move as the bones aligned.

I have been to chiropractors and massage therapists who can work muscles and bones into place, but this was movement in my spine with no manipulating contact. It was all Albert speaking with his God-given authority. A year later, I still have complete use of my shoulder.

With no prior introduction, Albert recognized my need to be healed. He prayed in the name of Jesus for it to happen and it did.

Amanda Traer, Jacksonville

I was diagnosed with scoliosis when I was 12 and started receiving chiropractic care by 14. I had a leg that was much shorter that resulted in having ribs out constantly in my back over the years and caused many other issues. In my 30's, I have had to see a chiropractor bi-monthly and get monthly massages to feel relief as I continue aging.

I didn't expect to ever be healed of this since surgery results are unknown. Someone told me to visit Albert when he was here in May. When he asked me to sit in a chair, I didn't know what to expect but trusted in God that something was going to happen. Next thing I knew, my right leg grew about 3 inches as he held it in his hands and prayed. He then addressed my scoliosis and praying in the name of Jesus, he felt down my spine. I felt some blood rushing to my lower back but couldn't tell until I stood up that it was straighter! I went to my chiropractor the next day and he was amazed at how different my back felt. He wasn't a believer in miracles of Jesus but is now. Especially since I haven't had to see him again!

Shea Griffin

I was privileged to meet with Albert at a meeting in Jacksonville Florida last year. Up to that point, I had been fighting my insurance company to get surgery performed on my sinuses.

Long story short, I told Albert of my condition and through the Holy Spirit, Albert prayed over my sinus condition and it immediately cleared up. Funny enough, my ENT doc called me back in to get a follow up for they had finally approved my surgery. Knowing that I was completely healed, I still went to the appointment and politely informed the doctor that I didn't need surgery after all because I was healed by the Holy Spirit. He did his cursory inspection and exclaimed that my sinuses were in perfect condition. "I couldn't have agreed more," I told him. I was then able to explain the miracle healing I received and that it was God working through Albert. Praise God!

Shea also met up with Albert for a men's breakfast at the Village Bread Cafe. His knee had been injured when he was only sixteen, and now in his 40's his ACL had been surgically removed. Albert ministered healing in Jesus's name and then told Shea to perform a full squat completely to the floor and stand back up again. He did so for the first time since his teens and was completely pain free. Now rather wide-eyed, Mike Elin remembered him saying that he didn't have an ACL to which Albert replied, "Well, you have a new one now!" Shea has since maintained an exercise program he never could have attempted until now – his cartilage is totally restored.

Peggy Alcorn, Jacksonville

Albert prayed over me for my migraine headaches, and it has been very successful. However, for several days after his prayers I experienced severe headaches again (I thought maybe it was Satan trying to butt in). The headaches have since stopped. Albert also prayed for my overall well-being since I also battle bi-polar disease, exhaustion, and muscle aches. Since his prayers, I have experienced a much healthier outlook all over. I thank Albert and the Lord for healing virtue.

Juhani Huotari, Finland, 2016

Testimony of Mr. Juhani Huotari, Voice of the Martyrs, Country of Finland. On June 6, Juhani thanked me for previously praying for him over the telephone for his terminal cancer and paralysis and to tell me his doctor confirmed his total healing.

Then in September Juhani flew down to visit Russell and me in Cuba, accompanied by a friend, Aki Miettinen, President of Voice of the Martyrs, Finland. It was a joyous and very meaningful visit.

Voice of the Martyrs in Finland has been a wonderful supporter of Russell's ministry in so many ways. They recently made a special donation of a lovely Ford SUV that allows the Colombian team to traverse the country so much better- using one vehicle instead of several.

Russell, Aki Miettinen (VOM Finland), Albert, and Juhani Huotari

Johan and Anna Candelin, Finland, 2017

This wonderful couple arrived in Colombia for a purpose. Johan as a director and an ambassador of two international organizations, First Step Forum and World Evangelistic Alliance, came to convey a Freedom Award on Russell Stendal. Honoring Albert as well, noting this effort was all about "Forgiveness – God's finger is there, not politics; and there is hope for Colombia not because man walked on the moon, but that God walked on earth and changed hearts."

Anna in turn also received an award, a beautiful gift of healing. Albert noted her walk and also the pain; so he ministered as he so freely does. With joy she walked upright, no longer in pain for the first time in years. Having travelled extensively, this will make life so much better.

Johan and Anna Candelin

Jeff Wingad, Salt Lake City

My adult son was born premature and had two different shoes sizes – God, through you, healed his foot – we instantly saw the shorter foot grow to same size. God, through you, healed my shoulder rotator cuff and I instantly felt my muscles grow back and crawl across my shoulder to completely heal.

You came to our house and prayed for Evie's elderly agnostic mom, which helped give her more time to live and accept Christ and have a real sweet transformation experience with God that inspired her to give Christian books and music to all her grandchildren prior to her death last November 2016.

Cindy Hilton, Florida

My first encounter with Bro. Albert was by telephone on the day he called to pray for me.

Bro. Bill and Sister Maryann Bennett from Hollywood assembly had heard that I was struggling with a diagnosis of diffuse large B cell lymphoma. I was undergoing chemotherapy treatment at the time sister Mary Ann called me to tell me they were praying for me. She also said that she had a burden that Bro. Albert would pray for me to be healed. She arranged a phone call between us since I was nowhere near him physically. He prayed for me to be healed, commanded the illness to be gone in Jesus' name. It was brief and to the point. The healing was in the hands of the Lord and I felt assured he was in control.

I did continue the chemo treatments for two more sessions. At that time, about the second session after Bro. Albert's prayer, I developed a bad fever that we could not get under control. The doctor put me on antibiotics. I took them a week without any improvement. Things looked worse, not better. I was put in the hospital and given heavy doses of IV antibiotics for five more days. Still no improvement. Then they started all the tests. They could not seem to find source of fever. Results from these tests changed things around very much, showing clearly the divine hand of God was at work. First of all, the CT scan of chest area seemed to show the lymphoma that was under the right arm appeared to be gone. Secondly, the heart test showed loss of heart function (when compared to pre chemo echocardiogram) and was attributed to one of the chemo drugs, therefore was stopped immediately. Thirdly, the pulmonologist called in by the primary doctor said that my lungs were being infiltrated by the chemo drugs as well and needed to be stopped because it was causing a condition called pneumonitis.

Lastly, an infectious disease doctor was called in. She said that the only thing it could be was the chemo port. She wanted it removed. Of course, the cancer doctors disagreed very adamantly. I listened to her and requested it be removed. The fever broke the same day it was removed, never to return.

I saw the sovereignty of God in this. He reached down and totally put a stop to everything, in such a divine way that even the doctors had no argument. They could not argue to continue treatment if it was hurting vital organs. They were forced to do a scan when they had no intention of doing any scanning since I wasn't even halfway through my chemo treatments. God even caused the port to be removed because (I believe) He knew I would not need any more treatments. God moved in such a way to declare my healing that no one could argue. It looked very bad for a few days but ended up being the revealing of my healing.

Trust in God always and he will divinely direct thy path! A pet scan done two months later has confirmed there is no indication of cancer. Thank you Bro. Albert for your simple but commanding prayer of authority, as well as all the precious brethren who prayed for me. We truly are a BODY, needing each member.

Josh Gorley, Hollywood, FL

Throughout 2015, I would notice short spells of numbness in my left hand. I thought it was from over working or I was just getting old – at 38. Not wanting to tell anyone, I grinned and kept on going. Later in the year, I started to notice pain before or after the numbness until one day in September, I awoke one morning in terrible pain. My wrist and hand were on fire. I didn't know what to do other than complain and complain I did. My wife, Mom and Dad would say, "Go to the doctor." And of course, I would put it off and lived with short battles with pain.

After the first of the year, the pain started spreading. One day it would be in my wrist, two days later it would be in my right ankle. The pain became so bad I would leave work, go home and sit on a couch, and not move. That's when I finally made a doctor's appointment.

I went to my primary doctor and told her what was going on. She took blood and scheduled another appointment. The results of the blood work read as if I had an autoimmune problem. My doctor set up appointments with several specialists who poked, prodded, shocked, squeezed and drained me, all while in crippling pain. Doctors mentioned several scary things such as: lupus, fibromyalgia, RA and others… and we need to keep testing and also see other doctors.

Then one day when I was outside, my favorite neighbor, Mr. Bennett, walked across the yard. We chatted and as always he said a prayer for me. He said he wants me to meet a friend of his, Bro. Albert who would be coming to town in a few weeks. Mr. Bennett started sharing stories about Albert; we already had a connection because of his work in Colombia, as I have a Colombian wife.

Albert arrived on Friday and we met at church later that night. Before the meeting, Albert talked with our family about what was going on with me. During church he called me to come forward for prayer. He asked God to take away the pain and the problem with the autoimmune disorder. As soon as he stopped praying there was a peaceful feeling all around me. The next day there was no pain and there has not been any pain since. I have not been back to the doctor, and that was almost a year now.

Thank you, Lord, thank you Mr. Bennett, and Mr. Albert. My life was definitely changed that night… God works miracles.

Over the next couple of days, while Mr. Albert was staying next door, I got to know him better. It was so nice to hear his stories and to ask him questions. I always look forward when Mr. Bennett says, "Albert is coming to town." He is a man of God.

The Bowerman's, Bowens Mill, October, 2016

The eye doctor informed us that Katie's eyesight was deteriorating badly. She was nearsighted and just received her new glasses to help her see. The first time that Brother Albert prayed for her, he asked her to open her eyes, and she commented that her sight was still blurry. Brother Albert then laid his hands on her eyes and prayed again for her healing. When he took his hand off and she opened them, her face lit up with such an expression of joy! It felt just like when I first held her in my arms when she was born. We were all greatly excited…she was beaming so bright. She had tears of joy and happiness, and could hardly contain herself. When I met her in the back of the room, she hugged me and asked, "What do I do with the new glasses?" I told her, "They would make a great hair band." She laughed at the fit I had when I found out how much they cost!

Later the next day we ran into Sister Maria Pasmino. Her account of the power of the Holy Spirit was that, as she laid her hand on Katie's back it was burning hot but wasn't burning her skin. Maria could feel the anointing running through her hand to Katie's body. (Brother Albert, earlier in the prayer session had requested that Sister Maria come up to help him in praying for the people in the room, because he felt the anointing over her the day before during the prayers.)

On another note, we took Abigail up for prayer for a cough she had had for over a month. Nothing was helping the issue. She hasn't had any problems with the cough since then. PTL!

I asked for prayer for my prostate; the symptoms were so much that I couldn't ignore them. I always thought that I wasn't claiming the issue but my dad is fighting the same thing and I didn't want to carry it too. I had no great sensation as Katie did, but I received healing and went about my way. Today I can tell you that I used to wake up three to four times a night to use the bathroom. Now I can often sleep through the night. Praise the Lord!

Thanks again for all yours and Sister Maryann's love for us and everyone you come in contact with. We are so very thankful to Brother Albert for being faithful to his calling-coming all across the country to our convention. He stood for hours both afternoons after the preaching services in the morning and prayed for so many who were beautifully healed. We were up front watching, and some were healed without him even touching them! He is a real servant of the Lord. Our love and bountiful thanks…

Katie

Bill Bennett, a Note on Albert's Ministry in Bowens Mill

Albert ministered to about a hundred adults and children in Bowens Mill with many experiencing divine encounters and miracles. This was also one of the first times that people actually received new cartilage in their knees! It seems that the anointing for this and cancer has greatly increased.

Albert said that this time in Bowens Mill was one of the highest anointing's he has ever experienced, and it carried over to his subsequent two days in Jacksonville. Part of this we believe is a testimony to the saints that were gathered. Midway through the first meeting a sister from CHOIR came and shared something the Lord spoke to her, which a little later we shared with everyone: "God said because these people love me so much, I am releasing a greater measure of healing." Love goes a long way and surely moves God's hand.

Raul Cardenas, Mexico

When Brother Albert Luepnitz prayed with me over the phone, both my legs and knees felt stronger. I even forgot all about my knee guards. My back now shows spine bones back in place. When in doubt, I can listen to the Holy Spirit whispering: will or will you not trust? The freedom of my body is a gift of the Lord. Thanks to your prayers! Everything else is back to normal. Glory!

A Process of Faith

Michele Clay, Ohio April 3, 2017

At the Bowens Mill Convention in October of 2016, Brother Albert Luepnitz was introduced to all of us. He announced that he would hold a session the following afternoon with all who were interested in gathering with him for the Lord's healing. I noticed right away that he is one of the most humble men I had ever met. I so appreciated his testimony and his manner of glorifying our Lord that I could listen to him for hours without end. He made me immediately comfortable and I felt that he was definitely operating through the Spirit of the Lord and not as those I had experienced while watching on television years ago.

That evening, I prayerfully wrote down a list of every symptom or ailment which I was experiencing, so if given the opportunity to ask for prayer, I wouldn't leave anything out. My list contained 12 items, 10 of which had been diagnosed by doctors. I had felt embarrassed and perplexed by so many health issues that have appeared in the last few years. At the time of the meeting with Albert, I was one month away from 61 years of age. I appear healthy and remain active; however, I was physically limited at times. I had no idea how I would approach Brother Albert with this list, but I trusted the Lord would provide a way if I was to do so.

At the session with Bro. Albert, he asked if there were any who had curvature of the spine to come forward and he would pray with us. Yes, that was on my list as Scoliosis. There were several that formed a line and I was one of those. I had visibly witnessed others before me and knew there were other things being healed and corrected in them. I was praising God in my spirit for what our Lord was doing in our midst. Some of us who had gathered were joining within ourselves in prayer with Albert as he was ministering to each one who had come forward. When it came time for Bro. Albert to pray for me, he asked me for what reason I needed prayer. Not knowing where to start, I simply handed him my list. He looked over my list and made a humorous comment about it. Albert's humor made me feel comfortable with him right away.

I knew the symptoms were real and I desperately wanted help from the Lord. Albert began praying for a few of the individual things on my list and then he handed back the list and prayed that the Lord would cover it all. Then he checked the curvature of my spine, and felt a knot on the back of my neck; and simply prayed for that knot to be healed. After praying, he told me to feel for the knot. I had known that it was there for many years, but when I reached back, *the knot was gone*! Tears of thanksgiving started to come. He sat me down in a chair and lifted both my feet from the floor. He showed me that one leg was shorter than the other, then said watch, and *God lengthened my leg*!

I stood aside to watch and pray for each of the others that had lined up after me. The line kept getting longer as we saw the healing power of God manifesting right before our eyes. As I stood there, I felt a very warm sensation come over me and immediately began to feel the muscle aches as I have always experienced the day following a chiropractor making manipulations. At that moment I knew the Lord was confirming to me that He had manipulated my neck, back and hips. Albert had only touched me, but God was making it clear that He had healed me through Bro. Albert. The soreness lasted for 3 days, and I have never been back to a chiropractor since.

Both my mother and maternal grandmother had been diagnosed and suffered with Alzheimer's. Bro. Albert prayed for me and I no longer have the fear of that disease coming upon me.

Also, I was diagnosed with Collagenous Colitis and had suffered for years with it either being in remission or out of remission. At the time that Albert prayed for me, it had been acutely aggressive for seven months. The aggressiveness immediately dissipated that day and within a few months, the symptoms were gone. I have had some days where the symptoms have returned and I've followed Bro. Albert's wise counsel, which I will talk about in a moment.

In addition, an endocrinologist had been watching several nodules in my thyroid, with two nodules in particular being quite large. They had been needle-biopsied as benign; however, due to the size, the doctor continues to monitor me for any change. He also put me on thyroid medication the month previous to Albert praying for me. After the prayer and taking two full prescriptions, I felt the Lord was releasing me from taking any more of the medication. (Please know that I do not condone doing this without your doctor's permission and/or having a clear Word from the Lord.) On a re-check with this specialist five months after prayer, the doctor said that I didn't need to take the thyroid medicine because my blood work showed my thyroid to be in the normal range. *Praise God! He did it!* An ultrasound will be done six months from this writing to look at the nodules still present. I am praying for God's continued healing to take place either by eradicating those nodules, or by stopping their growth. Also, a bone scan for osteoporosis will be done, but it was on my prayer list and I will trust God.

Bro. Bill Bennett, a friend of Bro. Albert's and instrumental in bringing Albert our way, told us that a Prophetic Word came, saying *"that Albert had been sent to us because of our love for The Lord!"* I continue to hold this in my heart, realizing that our love moves the hand of God.

Albert gave us wise counsel that it may take some time for healing to manifest or remain. If any symptom or pain comes after prayer, he instructed us to be quick to say, *No!* He also told us, *"Don't doubt and be persistent."* Yes, I have had to use Albert's counsel more than once, and also trust God as I wait for His complete healing of body, soul, and spirit.

The following day, a woman handed Albert a list and he lovingly mentioned the long list "someone" had given him the day before. I realized that I am no longer embarrassed or anxious about the many diseases and conditions that were confirmed by doctors. God allowed that list and I have kept it in my Bible as a reminder to me that He has touched every single item.

The greatest healing was accomplished in my soul. I have peace concerning the physical ailments and all fear is gone. They were for God's glory and to show me that I can bring all to Him. The Lord will walk through it with me or He will completely heal and restore. Either way, I am in Him or He is in me. All is good with His peace in my soul. Another aspect that has taken place since our time with Albert is "How I pray for others." There has been such a release of faith to ask for healing in body, soul, and spirit, as hands are being laid on them; and also if there is a need to bind or cast out anything that the Lord may reveal.

I am so very thankful and grateful for God bringing Bro. Albert to us to once again show us His love and that we have such a brother in whom we can rejoice in God's gifts through him. We will hold him in our hearts and pray often as he continues on as God's ambassador.

God's Ambassador

Brother Albert is an *experience*. "A special agent of God." Many see him as a healer, and he is. However, he is so much more – he is *God's instrument for divine encounters*. It is difficult to capture him in words, but let the following statements give you somewhat of a picture:

- When Russell Stendal wanted us to meet him, he simply said, "Albert is the humblest man I know." How about that for an introduction!

- Ivan, the second in command of the FARC in Colombia, who was a vital part of the Peace Process that was negotiated in Cuba, was a hardened Marxist killer. His simple testimony: "It wasn't the word spoken, or the miracles that turned me to Christ, it was you!" An epistle read of all men impacted this guerrilla, who now may be an evangelist.

- A prophetic word through Mrs. Vick at a meeting in Longview, Texas in 2016 proclaimed, "I am proud of you Albert for you have been obedient in everything I have told you to do." Well done faithful servant, a word of encouragement from his Father!

We can only complement these tributes with but a few thoughts on this unusual man who bears many gifts and much fruit. Albert loves everybody, particularly the unlovely – that's the fruit God's love has brought forth. For his many gifts, Albert gives all the glory to God, while keeping his ego under – no small feat. So many brethren see only the gift of healing, thus miss the Godly character, which carries wisdom and brings forth a prophetic voice.

Many read his book and concentrate on the healings which are certainly marvelous. However, the close reader will realize it also carries a much needed message of inner healing. This comes from many years of discerning and applying God's word. In addition, Albert sees healing from many viewpoints. One, this was the means, the power God used to open the hearts of the FARC to the Gospel. Two, he sees the need to prepare hearts for God's touch. Three, a wonderful approach to open up the gate of faith by examining legs – when lengthened people tend to believe and are then able to join with his faith to go further. This visual act also encourages others.

Albert is a teacher of applied truth and an encourager. When he prays, it is simple, direct and with authority…as God's ambassador, Albert *always prays in the powerful name of Jesus.*

Put simply, Albert lives Jesus!!

Now, his keen desire is to take God's Kingdom to the inner cities of America. And at 91 years, he is still ready and able. Albert is a true friend and our fellowship has adopted him. Lord, may you multiply Albert's strength and his anointing.

– Bill Bennett, Hollywood, FL

Visions and Prophetic Words

Virginia Cobern, January, 2016

New doors are opening, tomorrow favors. When you enter a country, city or town they will see you as a gift that God has sent.

New doors are opening internationally this year. You will minister to individuals who will carry your message to the head of their nation

I have opened a door to a place that you have not stepped into yet. I have put into you a God given message you are to convey and he will use you to make a change in government.

What I have for you will take a lot of effort. I am going to use you with ministers that are off beat, that are missing the mark, but I will use you to change them. Some will not comply, but they will go down but the rest will say whatever it takes.

I am giving you dreams and visions of the end times. You say you are an old man but your walk is not over. I go before you. I am the one that keeps you safe. You are very important in my eyes says the Lord.

Maria Doherty, November, 2016

"God showed me a light house, the ministry you are going to start is like a lighthouse.

As it goes around, the light flashes every few seconds. I saw throngs of children and families being drawn to the light. Each time the light circled around the hundreds and hundreds of children grew and grew…like waves with each turn of the light. Also with each turn of the light the waves of people healed were exponential.

The lighthouse was a center, drawing people into being healed from addictions to drug, alcohol abuse and much more.

God showed at first there was only the one lighthouse but soon lighthouses were popping up all over the United States and soon the whole country was filled with lights that were touching the outer edges of the next light.

Later, God added to the vision for Albert. Most of the children were of darker skinned nature, but there was a little boy …a Caucasian boy, round face, big eyes and cutest pudgy cheeks, named Samuel or Samson. He was trying to get to the center of the hundreds of people. No one was able to get closer since so many people were in the vision, but the people simply parted and this little boy walked up."

Albert, February 12, 2017

This morning as I was thinking of the yesterdays in an Indian village in Colombia, they were going to give me a love offering. They had no money, but were putting what they had in a bucket: their pen, comb, watch, bells, etc. Russell caught it and told them it was okay-"Albert did not require an offering."

What followed was over twelve hundred Indians were healed in less than an hour as I prayed for them – many were not even touched. The only words spoken were, "in the name of Jesus."

Why did this happen? They were willing to give the only thing they had; and my message was, "just give and submit yourself." And they did.

The dirt floor was covered with Indians in all sorts of

positions, loudly praising God, giving him thanks for their blessing and healing.

I closed my eyes, and like dreaming, I saw city gang members, in small numbers, doing the same as I ministered.

Albert, February 26, 2017

I awakened yesterday morning about 3 a.m. Within minutes these are the words I heard, "I want you to know why I told Russell to use you before going to Cuba the first time in January 2013. I had the minister in April 2013 tell you: Albert, this says the Lord, you are the only one I have trained to do what I want you to do in Cuba, so you cannot quit."

This is what He told me: "The training was, after you received the fullness of the Holy spirit you not only received the necessary training 'operating in the gifts of healings,' but to hear, to recognize my voice and follow my instructions…very necessary 'gifts' to do the job I needed you to do."

I cried for a while and recalled the words the lady spoke in September 2016, "Albert, I am proud of you because you followed my instructions."

Albert, March, 2017

This gave me added confidence and assurance that God was going before me and would make the way clear just as He did in Cuba for those years with the FARC guerillas.

In Retrospect

As Albert has pondered the last thirty-three years in Colombia, and particularly the last nine years in ministry alongside Russell, it is his wish to leave you with hindsight and prophetic foresight. This, of course, holds true for Colombia, but also portends the ministry going forward – both in Colombia and the inner-cities, as well as the ripple effects it will have for the Kingdom of God elsewhere.

Hindsight: Having ministered to all segments of society, such as simple believers with their only allegiance being to Jesus has allowed the Lord to impact the whole. They have kept the focus on Him and away from sides and ideologies, including religious, secular, military, FARC, Indian, communist, etc.

Jesus, the Prince of Peace, was their Friend and they were his ambassadors. Each endeavored to faithfully hold to a three-fold cord that was not broken – truth, faith and love.

Somehow, Jesus in his infinite wisdom made his heart known: *"with Him, we saw ones not as they were but rather as they could be."* Therefore, Albert and Russell could identify with the Apostle Paul and realize that, for such a cause we, as prisoners of Jesus Christ for you Colombians, ministered grace toward you, Ephesians 3:1-2

Prophetic Foresight: We are witnesses to the deep workings of His Spirit in these people; and have the assurance that Colombia will be a beachhead for the Gospel of the Kingdom. The believers have experienced the reality of life in Christ and this fruit will be shared. Ivan, one of the FARC guerrillas could well become an evangelist – out of his own mouth he has said, "All I can think about is souls." All but one of their peace delegation made a commitment to Jesus.

Many of the military leadership are passionate and true patriots. They are an excellent trained cadre, about 500,000 strong. Upwards of 20 to 30% of the Army are believers. They are *"salt and light."* Recently they introduced a new manual for the military, in concert with something called *The Damascus Doctrine.* This is an ambitious project inspired by the conversion of Saul of Tarsus, a persecutor of Christians, who became the Apostle Paul, a defender of the faith. He lost his sight and recovered it at the hand of Ananias in Damascus. Their objective is to convert from a war footing to a peace effort and help bring restoration and reformation to a hurting nation. In their manual they actually confirmed Albert's mantra that the way of forgiveness – God's way – is the only way and further stated that "peace is the victory."

Paradoxically, this reminds us of Jesus Santrich who related to Albert that, *"he now has new eyes inside and sees things totally different."* Heretofore, a worldly view but now a Kingdom view. It certainly appears that there will be two parallel forces diligently working on behalf of the people of Colombia. The one will be given to encourage and foster a time of restoration and peace to a torn society. The other will be to present the spiritual: grace and truth through lives that have been enlightened by the

Gospel which will produce true freedom. This represents a battle for the soul of Colombia, to be won on the battlefield of faith.

And it is no coincidence that these two missionary states-men, Albert and Russell, are engaged along the way, having collectively "poured out" eighty plus years of their lives for such a people. The very meaning of their s portend to God painting a picture. Albert's name means *"Noble with a character quality of Man of Honor."* Albert is a twenty-five year Army veteran who was converted at age 55 from a hardened military cop to a missionary with a heart for Colombia! At 91 he is still saluting the Captain of his Salvation and carrying out orders. Ironically, the military has a dossier on Albert in which he is known as the "Paul of Colombia."

And Russell Martin's name means *"Warlike one with a loyal spirit and wise discretion."* His entire family – parents, wife and children along with their mates have given their lives to the betterment of Colombia. All are fully engaged in living out the Gospel and daily contributing to making their homes a place for dialogue, for care, and for hospitality. Their min-istry efforts include a broad spectrum of creative expressions: radio, music, literature, film, teaching, and conversations, with one-on-one special times. Because Russell has been a friend to thousands, his home is a revolving door of people coming and going all day long.

These actually are chosen ones, true servants who are ambas-sadors for the soul of this nation. All have been miraculously preserved through these war-torn years. Like the Prophet Daniel, they have been given skill and understanding for such a time as this (Daniel 9:22). And like the Apostle Paul they possess a unique calling, beautifully expressed in the book of Ephesians, ***For this cause***, *I bow my knees unto the Father of our Lord Jesus Christ, Of whom the whole family in heaven and earth is named, That he would grant you, according to the* *riches of his glory, to be strengthened with might by his spirit in the inner man.* (Ephesians 3:14-16).

They have served a cause bigger than themselves. It will take those of like minds to join together and selflessly pursue the *Damascus Doctrine* for Colombia to become the nation God has purposed – to lead the way, a beacon of peace and freedom for all of South America.

Russell and Albert are ordinary men whom God is using in extra ordinary ways. Both embody a secret shared by all true saints; be an instrument of peace in His hands and live to the glory of God alone.

– The Editor

Photograph of Albert, Russell's dog, and Russell. The dog was healed of deformed hip joints when Albert prayed for him.

My Friend Albert

I have shared many valuable and unique experiences with Albert Luepnitz over the past ten or so years. He is an outstanding example of a faithful and humble servant of the Lord who has used his gifts wisely in the service of the Kingdom of God without seeking personal gain.

Many memorable things have happened while Albert has been a guest at our home in Bogota. There was the time when a lady with a severely deformed foot arrived for prayer. Albert told her to take off her shoe and sock and to put her foot up on our living room coffee table. Then, Albert turned his back on the lady and invited all of us to gather around her for prayer. I came into the room at that precise moment and witnessed when God healed the lady while Albert's back was turned and no one had even begun to pray.

We have seen many miracles over the phone while I have been in the emergency room or intensive care ward with my hand on someone seriously ill and Albert has prayed over the phone with immediate results. There is a timing of the Lord to these events as he brings things together. My son, Dylan, has a 150-pound Alaskan Malamute that developed shoulder problems. Eventually, the dog was in a lot of pain and didn't even want to get up. I called Albert and the dog was healed instantly.

A couple weeks ago a Colombian senator arrived at our house with an Army colonel that had serious pain and complications from a botched surgery several years earlier. As I was thinking of calling Albert, and picked up the phone, it rang because Albert was calling me! He prayed and the colonel received a beautiful healing.

On January 3, 2013 I found myself on an airplane together with Albert flying to Havana, Cuba. We had spent the past four years accompanying the Colombian Peace Process between the FARC rebels and the Colombian Government. God has used Albert on many levels. There have been numerous miraculous healings to individuals on all sides of this conflict along with prophetic messages to specific leaders (including to the President) that have been sharp and to the point as Albert has trumpeted the message that peace must be accomplished "God's way or else."

Great victories were made in the discipleship by Albert and myself of key guerrilla leaders. The head FARC ideologue recently declared his faith to a Colombian senator: "I want you to know, that I am a Christian." Ivan, the second in command of the FARC said, "From now on I must be a pastor because everywhere I turn I see so many lost sheep." The significance of these statements is nothing short of a miracle as God is changing hearts, trying to conduct their lives "God's way," and thus fulfilling the Word from the Lord by Albert in 2013.

God's way is to forgive and forget. The only way to do this is through a change of heart. When hardened warriors received Albert and myself, God got his foot in the door and began to change their hearts. We have had the joy of watching a fifty-two year conflict be brought to a close and the peace accord finally entered into effect on December 1, 2016. Now, a growing number of those who were successful in war have come to the feet of the Lord Jesus and are becoming increasingly successful in promoting His peace.

– Russell Stendal, December 7, 2016

Awards from the Military

Colonel Pedro Javier Rojas representing the Colombian military and the government came to meet with Albert at Russell's Bogota residence in late January 2017. He and his wife were very gracious, and Javier mentioned that he had been selected to present a unique award to him. His coming was particularly heartwarming as he had been one that Albert had previously prayed for over the phone at Russell's request. He was wonderfully healed. Now, before proceeding with his mission, Javier asked if he would also pray for his lovely wife who was in pain. Gladly Albert took her before the Lord and she was healed of the back pain after one leg that was two inches short grew out right before her eyes.

Then the colonel explained his actual reason for coming and apologized for being late. It seems that he was preparing to leave for China as the military adjunct to the Colombian Embassy. He related to Albert's surprise that the military had a dossier on him and also that he had become known as "The Paul of Colombia." This was particularly fitting because of the award that he was sent to present. Then he read from the passage of scripture concerning the Apostle Paul who was being referred to in the newly adapted military manual that was just released. It includes and explains their new directives and mission. This has a lot to do with peace and human rights as the stated mission of the military. He had autographed a copy of the manual and in giving it to Albert explained that he was lovingly considered a special agent, "A Paul" who has ministered mightily to our troops over the last thirty-three years. It seems that Albert's message of forgiveness and the gifting to affect divine encounters and miracles have made a significant impact on Colombia.

Javier said this also resulted in his being able to engage in the peace treaty efforts to help bring about a very illusive victory for all of Colombia. Then the colonel with tears in his eyes proceeded to remove from his pocket a beautiful gold medallion which prior to now had only been given to Russell Stendal. It seems that the Colombian army recently changed their entire doctrine or code of conduct that governs every person and every unit in order to adapt to the new period of post conflict. The new doctrine is named "Damascus," inspired by the conversion of Saul of Tarsus. So Albert and Russell were being awarded this special Damascus Gold Medallion for their successful work leading to the conversion of many. They continue to receive many testimonies from soldiers and police whose lives have been transformed, all glory to God.

During his last visit in March, he was again stunned when Russell brought a group of ten generals to meet with him. Albert ministered healing to some and then with sincerity, passion and tears they proceeded to convey their deepest thanks. Each branch presented a medal along with an honorary three-star general status! This was a testament from the Colombian military for sending us to their country. They too were in essence giving glory to God the only way they knew how, by gratefully acknowledging His ambassadors.

To be identified with a military that has bravely served their country was a humbling experience. And for Colombia to relate to Paul's example by deploying the term Damascus, spoke beautifully to their new mission of dedicating themselves to peace and freedom.

– The editor

Colonel Rojas presenting the Damascus Medallion to Albert.

Damascus Medallion

The one from the Army is an honorary three-star general (they have suns instead of stars). The one from the Air Force was an honorary three-star general. The one from the police is a special teaching award accompanied by a special cap that only police generals are allowed to wear. Recently, another award came from the Navy as an honorary Rear Admiral.

The Jesus Challenge

Thanks for taking the time to share our thoughts and divine encounters with you. I believe the Lord would have me leave something special with you – just think of it as a *Jesus Challenge*.

We both know that Jesus is "no respecter of persons." We also know that the Bible says that each believer has been given "a measure of faith." With all my heart I believe He would be most pleased if you would decide to answer the call to walk by faith, responding to the promises of God and bless many in Jesus' name. We are to be ambassadors, representing Him to those in our circle of family, friends, and ones whom we come in contact with in our everyday walk. The scripture says that we are to be, *epistles read of all men*.

Will you also do your part in bringing in His Kingdom upon the earth? When Jesus was resurrected and ascended to the Father, He sent back the Holy Spirit to abide with us, empowering us to live by faith. We have become a vital part of the family of God and are privileged to spread the Gospel, the good news of the Kingdom. With a "mustard seed of courage," we can allow Jesus to move through us by faith and affect the world around us.

"Jesus is my friend and I am His ambassador" is my simple testimony. Almost forty years ago God healed me, delivered me, and called me to go and do likewise – to make a difference to all I came in contact with. All I had to do was give myself into His hands, stay clean and be encouraged each day to allow Jesus to move through me by that same Holy Spirit. You too can *Embrace Adventure with Jesus* and be a part of a cause that is bigger than all of us, yet is within our reach. Near the end Jesus spoke these words to all who are called by his name: *Let not your heart be troubled, ye believe in God, believe also in me*, John 14:1.

Faith steps over fear and doubt. You do believe in God; the need now is to believe Jesus will answer in agreement with the promises of His word. Remember, God is no respecter of persons and with Jesus you are well able, if you stay clean and step out. When I took those early steps, I had no idea what God was going to do. But with each day, each month Jesus came to affirm my simple faith, bringing divine and prophetic encounters.

We will soon have a booklet to encourage believers to stay on the path to victory; and will make it available via email, if you are willing to accept *The Jesus Challenge*. Whatever the issue, the problem or the need is, take them to Jesus. You can make the difference.

See yourself in the drawing depicted on the next page.

Be an ambassador by faith in Jesus name...

Albert: aluepnitz@aol.com
Bill: bbennett@connections.com

The Jesus Challenge

Soli Deo Gloria

About the Author

A lbert W. Luepnitz is ninety-one years old and has been coming to Colombia at his own expense every year for the past thirty years to pray for wounded and sick soldiers, guerrillas, and civilians. A retired special agent from the US Army Criminal Investigation Division with years of experience as an investor in real estate, he holds a Bachelor of Education degree from the University of Omaha with a major in Criminal Investigation. In 1981, he was diagnosed with an incurable, service-related back condition, however, when a woman prayed for him and spoke healing in the name of Jesus, he received a miracle healing and was baptized in the fullness of the Holy Spirit. She spoke two prophecies over Albert: that the Lord was going to use him in the gifts of healing (1 Corinthians 12); and that the Lord would use him as an ambassador of peace to nations. Albert is a widower and lives in Longview, Texas.

Albert Luepnitz
NS40 Lake Cherokee
Longview, TX 75603
aluepnitz@aol.com

The Hidden Agenda expands on the ministries of Russell Stendal and Albert Luepnitz, in Colombia and Cuba.

Marxists guerillas, right-wing paramilitary, and the Colombian government each have their own agenda. Who would have guessed a meeting of the minds would take place under the helpful auspices of communist Cuba? And that these battle-scarred leaders would give reporters and missionaries the opportunity to challenge some of their core philosophies and even pray with them?

During the often intense negotiations, it becomes obvious that even the most hardened individuals can have a change of heart. Previously seen only as men to be feared, these powerful leaders are now turning to the only one who can provide lasting peace – the Lord. The Stendals have witnessed Army generals having daily prayer and distributing Bibles to their troops, guerrilla commanders requesting and receiving prayer for healing, paramilitary commanders asking their many victims, one by one, to forgive them, and many other powerful demonstrations of what the Lord does through those willing to love their enemies. God's agenda is winning, and we watch in awe.

Available where books are sold.

American bush pilot Russell Stendal, on routine business, landed his plane in a remote Colombian village. Gunfire exploded throughout the town, and within minutes Russell's 142-day ordeal had begun. The Colombian cartel explained that this was a kidnapping for ransom and that he would be held until payment was made.

Held at gunpoint deep in the jungle and with little else to occupy his time, Russell asked for some paper and began to write. He told the story of his life and kept a record of his experience in the guerrilla camp. His "book" became a bridge to the men who held him hostage and now serves as the basis for this incredible true story of how God's love penetrated a physical and ideological jungle.

How did this incredible true story affect Russell? "At first my mind went wild with thoughts of revenge and violence. Then, after a while, I was able to see through their attempt to break me down and brainwash me. I started making a determined effort to throw all their stories and dramas out of my mind and not to let my thoughts dwell on them at all. I would trust God that He would take care of my wife and I would close my mind to my captors' input. I decided to think about positive values instead."

Available where books are sold.